BOY TO MAN,
MAN TO SON

CARNELL MOSES

Scripture quotations taken from The Holy Bible, New International Version®, NIV®. Copyright © 1973, 1978, 1984, 2011 by Biblica, Inc. Used with permission of Zondervan. All rights reserved worldwide. www.zondervan.com

Printed in the United States

ISBN   979-8-9948122-0-4 *paperback*
        979-8-9948122-1-1 *ebook*
        979-8-9948122-2-8 *hardcover*

Library of Congress Control Number: 2026903266

To the memory of my mother

Contents

Author's Note

The stories and events shared in this book are depicted to the best of my recollection. Some of the names have been changed to protect the identity of those individuals. Some of the names have been captured to pay homage to their positive and significant impact on my life.

As a fundamentally private person, I had an assortment of feelings about sharing my personal story so openly. However, I felt called to offer the nuggets of inspiration and hope that emerged from those years. Whilst you may or may not resonate with the details of my story, do your best to internalize them as a perspective you might not have previously considered.

PROLOGUE

Love is the most lasting legacy.

Growing up, I really never heard the word legacy used in my household. The focus for the most part was on surviving and unfortunately, the very principle of legacy had to take a back seat. Notwithstanding, I do believe we must be intentional about making and leaving a legacy. Legacy is the impact a person has made with their possessions after they have transitioned from their time on this planet as a living, breathing human being. It is being remembered for what you have done to touch the lives of others in some distinct and pronounced way. One thing I am certain of: My parents and grandparents left a rich legacy of familial love.

I want to be clear: In my mind, possessions can be both tangible and intangible. Fulfilling your life's purpose—whatever that may be—creates a consequential contribution to society. Even working to define what your purpose *is* sends you well on your way to leaving a legacy. I often ask myself, "How will my children's children know I was on this earth? How will they speak of their grandfather's contribution?" That self-talk often presses me to be deliberate about the ways in which my name will be carried forward after I am gone. I hope to leave a legacy that is both positive and profound, and a benefit to others in some real way.

Leaving a legacy is a tremendously selfless act of love with a biblical historicity. Allow me to share that context and make the connection, in case you missed it or are not familiar. In fact, I missed it myself until recently. Intriguingly, it comes from a story about a man whose name I share—Moses.

In the book of Exodus, Moses leads the Israelites out of Egypt with detailed scripts of provision from God. But Moses was a survivor who was not supposed to be a significant figure at all. Pharaoh, the king of Egypt, had exploited the Israelites with an oppressive hand and enormous subjugation and servitude. Egypt profited significantly from slave labor like this for years. Over time, however, the Israelites grew significant in number, and at a certain point, Pharaoh ordered midwives to destroy any baby boy that the Israelites delivered. With this official order in place when Moses was born, his mother placed him in a basket and released him into the Nile River. As it turned out, Pharaoh's daughter discovered the basket with Moses in it. While he was supposed to be a slave or dead, Moses instead grew up as royalty.

Eventually, Moses left Egypt after committing a murder, defending a Hebrew who was being beaten by an Egyptian. Moses stayed on the run for many years, until an angel of the Lord appeared to him in the flames of a fire that did not burn up the bush it consumed. Through the fire, the Lord said to Moses, "I have indeed seen the misery of my people in Egypt. I have heard them crying out because of their slave drivers, and I am concerned about their suffering." (Exodus 3:7) God wanted to send him to Pharaoh to lead the Israelites out of Egypt. The most illuminating part of this encounter is when Moses complained that he could not approach Pharaoh—not because he was on the run, but because he had a speech impediment. Being no respecter of persons, God commanded

Moses to go anyway and assured Moses He would be with him and serve as his mouthpiece. For all of us who have disabilities and hang-ups, God can still use us all. What's more, our disabilities and hang-ups do not negate us from leaving a legacy. In fact, I would suggest that they propel us even more, noting the touch of a tender heart impacting others even in our own condition—yes, touching lives in a distinct and pronounced way. God can still use us regardless of our condition, and He still gets His Glory at the same time.

When Moses and his brother Aaron approached Pharaoh, they made a declaration on behalf of the God of Israel: "Let my people go, so that they may hold a festival to me in the wilderness." (Exodus 5:1) Pharaoh, having a hard heart, refused to release the Israelites, and his sequential stubbornness led to a series of plagues. First, the Nile River turned into blood, the water becoming undrinkable. Then there was a plague of frogs all over the land, followed by a surge of gnats, then a circus of flies. Next came the death of livestock, then soot that caused festering boils to break out on people and animals. After all this, Pharaoh's heart was still hard, so the worst hailstorm that had ever fallen on Egypt came next, destroying all the flax and barley. Then locusts covered the land, darkness fell for three days, and the final act against Pharaoh and Egypt was a plague on the firstborn male. Whether human or livestock, they all succumbed to death. At this, Pharaoh had finally had enough and ordered the Israelites to get out of Egypt.

God led His people out of Egypt with a pillar of cloud by day and a pillar of fire by night, and they went on to spend forty years in the wilderness. Pay attention to this closely: The

Lord made provisions for the Israelites during this time *in the desert*, including bread which they called manna. At the Lord's direction, Moses saved a container of manna so that future generations could see the provision the Lord gave them in the wilderness after He brought them out of Egypt. Eventually, this container was placed in the Ark of the Covenant. (Hebrews 9:4) There is the connection to legacy that we are looking for: The Ark with the gold jar of manna served as a legacy of God's provision whilst wandering in the wilderness. It was a powerful punctuation of God's providence, reminding the Israelites of His infinite wisdom and leaving a lasting and memorable endowment of His love.

In the same way, as much as humanly possible, we must make provisions for others so that future generations reap the benefit of that provision—especially when the wilderness rears its head. When the future generation gets to recall and reclaim that love, it may be what carries them through during their own difficult times.

If you have not yet read the book of Exodus, I encourage you to have a read. I often tell my children—and I will now challenge you—to take time to see all that the Bible has to offer, and I can promise you will not be disappointed. You will discover as you read that, even with all the things that occur on earth today, there is nothing new under the sun. The Bible speaks to some element of all that we see around us. Search the scriptures for yourself to validate or find the truth. I did not begin this pursuit in earnest until I became a young father and husband. Only then did I begin to search for truth, in an effort to understand the meaning of my hardships and failures.

As my appetite for reading Scripture grew, so did my desire to leave the kind of legacy that I saw within its pages. That was the first reason I set out to write this book—to offer a window to truth and love in a way that might touch someone's life and leave a legacy of my own.

The second reason for this book is to provide inspiration and a measure of hope for those who have experienced trauma in its various forms. Life, in a large measure, has a lot to do with rebounding from losses. The loss of a mother or father, the loss of a child, the loss of a family structure, the loss of the innocence of a child, the loss of freedom, the loss of a job, the loss of a relationship. As you can see, and perhaps know all too well, losses come in various forms. Experiencing trauma, in some ways, is inevitable. It is perfectly okay to mourn these setbacks, while still knowing that the trauma we face is not the end of the story. I am always inspired when I see human beings deploying strength, resilience, discipline, and persever-ance amidst their troubles and pain. We are resilient, getting knocked down and back up, over and over again.

There is a wonderful connection between hope and resil-ience. Hope is the substance of things yet unseen, with the belief that these things will be made seen. It is a powerful phe-nomenon. But hope without resilience and faith is a fantasy, in my view. It is not based in reality. Whilst I hope for a thing to be made seen, am I resilient enough, with an active faith, to see that thing through to manifestation?

A distinguishing part of my passion and purpose in life has become inspiring hope when there seems to be none. Over the years, I have coached youth sports, mentored young men in juvenile detention centers, and mentored young men in alternative learning schools. Each time I am engaged in these efforts, my desire is to inspire, motivate, and impact hundreds if not thousands of young men toward a path of peace and fulfillment in their lives, regardless of their lot in life. (Notice I did not say lead young men to a path of *happiness*.) Out of random curiosity, I recently searched my historical log of text messages, both incoming and outgoing. I found the word "hope" used more times than I could count. These references were astounding to me, reinforcing my dependence on and hope in the God we trust. With healthy hope, we can always go another day—one step at a time.

> *"Therefore, since we have been justified through faith, we have peace with God through our Lord Jesus Christ, through whom we have gained access by faith into this grace in which we now stand. And we boast in hope of the glory of God. Not only so, but we also glory in our suffering, because we know that suffering produces perseverance; perseverance, character; and character, hope. And hope does not put us to shame, because God's love has been poured out into our hearts through the Holy Spirit, who has been given to us." (Romans 5: 1-5).*

This book offers my own context of hope and resilience—that of a young boy raised by a single mother, stumbling into manhood, then dipping into this mixed bag of experiences, both good and bad, to offer nuggets of wisdom to my own children. As for the timing of this book, given the benefit of life experiences that I've been granted, it felt clear to me that the time was now. Oftentimes, men are too manly to outwardly express the words "I love you" to their sons, consequently leaving a vacuum for unsavory characters to fill. Regardless of the state of our relationship, at any given time—from youngsters to adults—my children have always heard the words "I love you" in the sound of my voice. Daughters and sons alike need to hear it.

I have been driven by both a sense of urgency to leave a legacy of written material for my children's children and to offer nuggets of hope to one person at a time. My hope is that this book will be equally useful for ladies and young women, including my daughter, to draw on its concepts and gain additional perspective. It is meant to be a window—a place you can pull ideas, insights, and inspiration from, no matter the size and shape of that window in relation to your own life. Whether you're a single father, a young boy or man, a single mother, or a grandparent raising a grandchild, it does not matter your lot in life; I do believe this book will have something to offer you.

I

EARLY IMPRESSIONS

Our decisions are
like the pouring of
raindrops; some will
fall on good ground
and some will not,
and throughout the
course of our life,
we will make a lot of
them. Then the sun
will rise and shine
on them all, and
thus make their final
determinations.

*A life is not defined by
circumstances, but rather
circumstances cultivate a life.*

On a crisp winter Sunday in December, I was born to Henry John Moses and Regina Gail Moses at Earl K. Long Medical Center in Baton Rouge, Louisiana. *Carnell Moses.* The name Carnell comes from an idea given to my mother from her sister, who later passed away in the early 1970s. The official documentation is that my mother's sister died from an apparent suicide because of the physical abuse she'd endured at the hands of her husband. However, some do believe she was shot by her husband and it was only made to look like a suicide. I can still remember bits of the commotion—she was locked in the bathroom, loads of police and family members were all around. The story has never been settled.

I make a point to mention that the hospital was a charitable hospital, noting that my parents had very little means for me to be born anywhere but a charitable hospital. They had no savings and no healthcare. It was a traumatic time for my parents and, by extension, traumatic to me, even though I was oblivious at the time.

And so it was for my mother. "Mama," as I affectionately referred to her, filed for divorce from my pops two years after I was born. Life-changing decisions—or in some cases, everyday mundane decisions—require evaluation from every possible and applicable angle, whilst ultimately coated in prayer.

Once the decision is made, you have to own it. No one will know your circumstances but you.

In my mother's case, I believe she calculated the cost of filing for divorce, young as she was, and concluded that it made no difference monetarily as she did not have much money to begin with. That there would be no real impact to her and her child's well-being and healthcare, as she had none to begin with. And that there would be very little change to her living conditions in the short-term and possibly the long-term as well. The divorce, I do believe, was compounded by outside influences and her unhappiness. Rightly or wrongly, she went through her decision-making process, owned it, and marched forward.

Before any opinions are formulated and metastasized, my mother was a strong, caring, firm, yet sensitive woman. A hard-working woman who believed in taking care of her responsibilities and obligations and did *not* believe in inconveniencing anyone. A plethora of teachable moments are yet to come from my mother, but one thing was for sure: She never took the high road to easy street. Whilst at times we may have been at or below the poverty line, the woman simply *worked*. Hard. I never saw my mother not work. This endearing quality molded my view of work—that is, that work is good. She had GRIT and toughness, GRIT being "Grinding Relentlessly In Thankfulness." These qualities enabled her to care for and protect those whom she loved.

I guess you could say my mother was proud, in the good sense of the word. Honest and loving, but a ruthless protector of those whom she loved. If you were to find yourself in a ferocious battle for survival, Gail Moses would be the woman you wanted in the foxhole with you, no matter how long the battle might take to win. She loved hard, and she loved deeply, with an enduring kind of love.

Mama and my pops were only married for a short period of time, but he had his own qualities. He was a well-known athlete in the track and field athletics circles, running track for Southern University and A&M College during my toddler years. He was regarded as one of the best hurdlers in the state. His college attendance was short lived, however; not long after the divorce, he left school and migrated to the state of Texas. Growing up, I spent the vast majority of my time with my mother, but my love for sports followed just the same as my pops. Eventually, I migrated to Texas as well, and it would prove to be an enormously prosperous state for me personally.

Whilst trauma comes in all its ugliest forms, nearly anything can be used to cultivate and improve your life and the lives of others, if you only allow it to.

Chase simplicity.

Our lives were designed with intimate detail—the connections of a massive number of nerve cells, DNA that are unique to each of us, all whilst being known in our mother's womb, set apart for a specific purpose before any of us were born. Even so, I do believe there is a simplicity to life. The simplicity of working hard and making a valued contribution to society, enjoying family and friends, embracing the leisure of our pastimes and whatever brings us joy... The pure and simple takeaway? Work to keep life simple.

Now, a single mother is raising a boy.

My mother didn't necessarily chase simplicity during these times; it was just a way of life. I guess I could say that the way we lived shaped my present endorsement of living a simple life. Keeping it simple will eventually afford you the opportunity to do what you want to do and enjoy doing, as opposed to only leaving room for what you have to do.

From my earliest memory, my mother had moved us to public housing. The suburban apartment complex in Baton Rouge, Louisiana, was made up of big, bright yellow, dilapidated apartment buildings.* You simply could not miss this apartment complex—especially from the main highway, which was only a block away. This location was prone to flooding,

---

*   This complex is partly the inspiration for the color of this book's cover.

though when there was a flooding event, we kids would simply play in it. With water rising to as high as a youth's knee, we'd sing out our sophomoric and wishful desires to escape the barrage of school stuff: "Rain, rain come today so that we could miss another school day."

Unequivocally, this apartment complex was known throughout Baton Rouge for its various incidents and overall roughness. I seemed to elude the more catastrophic incidents, some of which occurred on a regular basis. Perhaps this could be attributed to not being a follower. Even at a young age, I was marching to my own rhythm. I had my own thoughts about who to mingle with and who to avoid, particularly if sports were not in play. I had this odd sense of self awareness, in that I could 'count the cost' or assess the risk of following a bunch of kids that were likely to get into some sort of trouble or have run-ins with the law. I did not always get it right, and I landed in hot water myself. But as a pre-teen growing up in public housing, I can say that I got it right more than I got it wrong. At least so much as it relates to being a follower.

Here is what I did not know to be true at the time, and what I am continuously learning now: As you count the cost of either standing alone or being influenced by unsavory characters, remember that the word 'no' has to be a part of your vocabulary, and there must be an accountability structure for you to adhere to. Fortunately, I had no problem with the word 'no.' Even as a pre-teen, my no meant no, and I had the ability to stand firm in it. Thanks to my mother, I also had the accountability factor in play. She was not about to take any of my shenanigans and would not hesitate with that rod of correction. To this day, I am begrudgingly appreciative for her hand of correction when it was necessary.

The character of a person is perhaps best illuminated through their energy. People will remember that energy—both positive and negative—and one such memory began in primary school at Lanier Elementary. The school principal, Mr. Crain, was a tall Caucasian man that was approachable, accepting, and bore an ever-present smile. Given that "once information becomes part of your long-term memory, you have access to it for a long time," Mr. Crain's wonderfully positive energy was a gift that I could not simply forget.[1]

I was absolutely loved by the teachers and school administrators. I am not exactly sure why. Was it because my mother would send me to school in suits, albeit on occasion and only inexpensive suits? Was it because I was incredibly respectful at such an early age? Was it because I was a no-nonsense kid? Was it because I had a learning disability that would ultimately require me to be held back a year? Perhaps, it was all of the above. The absolute answer eludes me to this day. Nevertheless, as I observed the school officials' positive actions toward me, I leveraged those potentially endearing characteristics as a way to subsist in public housing. For instance, my attire was always just a cut above my peers', and while I gave respect, I also demanded respect in return.

As I continue to paint my own reality of the environment I grew up in, I am, of course, worried you might judge me for the impoverished nature of my upbringing. Please do not misjudge the beautiful learnings I gained from that time. However, neither can we ignore the fist fights occurring on a regular basis, usually centered around bruised egos. At that time, we did not use firearms to settle our differences, but rather used our fists—and some, occasionally, used knives. Then there were the "old-school gangstas" hanging out with 40-ounce bottles of beer in brown paper bags, twisted at the top. Just about every apartment home was led by a young woman, with no fathers present. Young pregnancies. An occasional stabbing. Young boys in handcuffs. The list goes on.

Alongside all of this, I came to love the competition inherent in sports. Sports are neither subjective nor biased. It is simply your desire to win versus your competitor's desire to win, and it is exhilarating. I took a real liking to basketball and actively participated in lots of open-play football as well. Interestingly enough, neither baseball nor soccer were played in my neighborhood in those years. Exposure is often a stimulus for invoking interests, but we had no real awareness of these sports, nor anyone to introduce us to them.

This introduces two words you will read throughout this book: exposure and appreciation. I had a real appreciation for public housing in the late 1970s—for struggles early in life, for understanding human behavior, for the value of seeing my mother work hard in an ethical way as a provider, the culmination of which would help me to avoid taking things for granted throughout my life. I could see and appreciate all the different dynamics surrounding me, and I innately started to observe those dynamics very closely. I started to sense when violence was on the horizon. I learned to be direct in what I wanted from my contemporaries, with fewer words but clear actions. I picked up on the notion of passive aggressiveness; I could hear what people were saying or not saying. I learned to see and feel the meaning of loyalty. I learned healthy fear. Between the tender ages of five years old and twelve years old, I found myself becoming more street wise, even as my interest and development in school began to slip. In this environment, I could say more by saying less, and that worked well for me.

As part of both my persona and my natural makeup, I had a "stone face," indifferent to the roller coaster ride of our times. My mother would often say that I was one of the most indifferent personalities she had ever had to deal with (never mincing or holding back her thoughts and words). Paradoxically, everyone I came in contact with knew when they had crossed the line with me in some way. If the eyes and a head nod alone could talk, I was saying a whole lot.

At the time, I could not articulate this newly developing seriousness or this odd presence I was growing into, but it was becoming clear to me that people received me with a level of cautiousness. And I leveraged it with all the kids in public housing. In return, they had an interesting level of respect, staying clear of the other side of my wrath. I was slowly beginning to understand the impact of my decisions—both good and bad—without allowing the dynamics of the environment to impact me negatively. In that way, my attitude of indifference was my way of keeping things simple.

Whilst exposure can be a gift, it can drive excitement and elevation, or it can elicit unhealthy behavior; the choice is ours.

I am not a trained psychologist. However, I would surmise that if I were confined to my home twenty-four hours a day, seven days a week, my growth and development would be limited by that meager existence. It would be psychologically calamitous. On the other hand, if I were exposed to the world outside of the confinement of my home—such as, exposure to other countries and cultures, different types of food, a variety of different sports, a great education—then it stands to reason that this exposure would drive as much excitement and elevation as the confinement would extinguish.

In this regard, I cannot help but think about the millions of individuals in jail or prison today. Our government and some in our society believe that the harsher the confined environment, the more likely a person will be changed for the better. In some cases, that confinement is less than or equal to a ten-by-ten cell, twenty-three hours a day, for seven days a week, with no exposure to anything or anyone. Is this wise? Again, I am no trained psychologist, but it seems counterintuitive to think that the worse a person is treated, the more likely we are to see the better side of that person. I am unable to make this make sense in any way, even in my own head. In fact, I would venture to say that the crueler and more inhumanely we treat a person, the more dogmatic, ruthless, and violent that individual is likely to become. Desperate people do desperate things.

Given that confinement leads to despair and exposure to growth, I sincerely believe that exposure to trades and crafts in these situations provides a bit of hope and a pull from said desperation. Rhetorically speaking, I believe we have a better chance of a person thriving after being released into society with a trade or a craft as opposed to having little or no exposure to anything outside of the jail or the prison cell itself. Do I really need to validate that thinking with data? It simply stands to reason—or perhaps that's just my unenlightened thinking and the hope that everyone can be reformed under the right circumstances and with the right exposure.

I will always remember and appreciate the exposure I was afforded from living in public housing. The outside world sees these living conditions as dire and lamentable. I felt that it provided the opportunity to engage with people who looked like me, though they had vastly different perspectives for our lot in life.

A good number of the other kids who grew up with me in public housing allowed the challenges of living in such conditions to affect their behavior. For example, if they saw violence, they too became violent. Street hustling became a normal and natural way of life for them. Some of those kids never had belief that their lives would get any better than their current condition—life was as good as it was ever going to be. Sadly, forty years later, multiple generations have lived in the same public housing. But it all depends on how you see your circumstances. For me, these humble beginnings became fuel to hope for more and to expect more from myself. It helped me to identify how I did not want to live life.

This particular kind of exposure taught me that you get out of life what you put in. My identity was shaped by the determination to work hard in order to never live life at or below the poverty line—marked by values of hard work, discipline, consistency, and occasionally making some good decisions. I credit my exposure to public housing as what drove me to always maintain multiple streams of legitimate income. I never succumbed to the stereotypes placed on me based on where I came from, knowing that I was the only person that had the power to give those stereotypes oxygen. That formative experience of living in public housing has kept me simultaneously humble and hungry for greatness!

Your attire accentuates your desires.

My mother exposed me to the best attire she could afford. Whether attending elementary school, visiting family, or going to the grocery store, my mother made sure I was always dressed to impress (on occasion, in inexpensive suits). It didn't matter if the attire came from K-mart, Payless, or a thrift store—she always made sure it was clean, fitted, and pressed just for me.

When I got older, I was considered a "preppy" dresser. My exposure to nice attire carried over several years later to my corporate life as well. Whilst our corporate attire was simply business casual, I was that guy—the one who stayed just a step above. My uniform for corporate life was a full suit, minus the tie. Then and now, whatever I've worn has been clean, fitted, and pressed. My mother exposing me to the importance of attire, demonstrating it without saying a word, was masterful.

Perception is reality, and in the end, my attire has always matched my desire to do impactful things in life.

Exposure shapes ideology—that is, how you see things, how you process things, how you react to things. If I cannot see a thing or participate in a thing, then how can I aspire to do or be that thing? Ultimately, exposure can be a conduit to finding purpose. Be open to exposure as opportunities present themselves, and you just might find why you were meant to be here on earth.

On the other hand, a lack of exposure can stunt personal growth, resulting in a narrow-minded worldview. If we are not careful, we can despise what we don't know or understand. For example, the lack of exposure to a complete family nucleus in my adolescent years was detrimental for me. I now fully understand that a healthy family structure is vital to our own health and well-being, vital to child rearing, vital to wealth building, and most importantly vital to operating in God's divine plan. Unfortunately, early in life I developed a single-minded view of how things should go and how relationships should be. The family structure was simply not looked upon in public housing as central, regardless of the societal or governmental construct. If it were, then perhaps I would have seen at least one married couple. This just didn't exist. As a result, I developed a hard, rough-rider view of relationships.

I have heard people say that marriage, in a large part, is a business decision and not necessarily about love. When I first heard this thought process, I thought it was interesting. Not wrong or right, I guessed. Just different. Unfortunately, it took the calamitous and awful sting of divorce to lead me to reflect on my own views on marriage and to process the significant portion that "value" (realized or unrealized) might play in a marriage or a relationship.

I now see marriage as both a love proposition and a value proposition. The longer two people are joined together, the more ups and downs there will be. In love and not in love—the relationship pendulum will swing as far as west is to east. When the pendulum swings out of love and one or both individuals stop receiving perceived value from their mate, separation or divorces hang in the balance. And as human beings, we will perceive a lack of value in something or in someone unless there is full transparency and a willingness by both parties to work through it—in love or not in love.

Fried foods, salty foods, and sweet foods were a staple in our community and in my mother's kitchen. Oh, and do not forget about the sugary products like soda pops and Kool Aid packs that were very much laced with sugar. Cheaper foods are normally the unhealthiest foods, and this is what folks in my community were most likely to purchase and consume. Hence, my palate was quite naturally normalized for these unhealthy foods.

Who could argue with grandma's big plate of salty greens, deep-fried chicken, and overly sweet candied yams? Unfortunately, many of my family members suffered from—and, in many cases, died from—heart disease and diabetes. Over the years, I had to retrain my taste palate for healthier choices. By no means was this easy.

For good or for bad, exposure is a big determinant in how we live our lives. We can only hope for exposure that improves and enhances our lives for the better.

A cousin from my mother's side of the family worked for a for-profit distribution carrier early on in his career. At the time, he was an industrious, young and idealistic individual. Whilst working for his employer by day, by night he had several small businesses, including a janitorial service and a car cleaning business. He married and started a family at a very young age, and by all accounts, he was the model of the American dream—a standout for our entire family, outside of my mother's brother, who passed away at a young age. However, his exposure to a world outside of his small town in Louisiana was nil.

He and I began to develop a close relationship in our early twenties. His first experience of another place outside of his small town was to visit me in Houston, Texas. I could see his fascination, along with being overwhelmed by the tall buildings, the highways and byways, and the various masterplan communities. Funnily enough, I remember taking him to a gas station, where I used my debit card at the gas pump. Once I was finished, he asked how I was able to pay for fuel without going inside.

One day, while on duty driving for the carrier, my cousin was in an accident. The window of the vehicle blew inside the carrier truck, cutting him in multiple spots on his arm, thus requiring medical stitching. Before he could fully report the accident to his employer, they were already making plans to release him from the company to mitigate their own exposure given the type and nature of the accident. The company was in full self-preservation mode.

Eventually, he would have to see a specialist in North Carolina, but there was one problem: He had never flown on an airplane before, and he was petrified of doing so. Working through the logistics of his location in Louisiana and mine in Texas, coupled with his limited functionality in only one arm, flying was the only option. He finally mustered up enough nerve to ask me to accompany him to North Carolina. He knew flying had become my preferred way to travel, and of course, I immediately agreed. This exposure to flying would open a whole new world for him. It resulted not only in a new perception of the area outside the state of Louisiana, but in an expanded worldview. He immediately began to understand he could do business and even vacation in other cities and states with the efficiency of traveling by air.

After we returned from North Carolina, he received the terrible news that his employer had officially released him from the company. Once again, he called me, this time to express his disillusionment and anger at the decisions made by his now former employer. I told him that he would be fine and everything would work out, but my comments only seemed to make him more discontented. However, these were not platitudes. My remarks came from a confident place. Over the years, I had observed how adept he was at operating his side businesses. With his ability to do strong-arm negotiations, the relationships he had cultivated and developed in his small town, and his ability to manage cashflow, I knew he would be fine.

Over the next decade or so, he went on to amass a small fortune. At its peak, his businesses eclipsed more than twenty million dollars in revenue annually. Much of this activity required him to do business in multiple states while collaborating with a host of other entrepreneurs. You guessed it—this also required air travel to effectively meet the demands and obligations of his growing business. That one moment of exposure elevated his capacity to deliver products and services to his customers and clients, ultimately elevating the financial security for his family beyond what he could have imagined.

Exposure is not a radical concept, but rather a revelational concept. By extension, discovery of passion and purpose is in revelational disclosure. Becoming an entrepreneur can only be revealed through exposure. Becoming a professional athlete can only be revealed through exposure. Becoming a pastor can only be revealed through exposure. The earlier a boy is exposed to various aspects of societal boons—sports and athletics, the arts, books, travel, and other cultures—the more likely it is that his passion and purpose will be discovered.

One might have the good judgment to know they should limit their intake of sugar, however, the longing for chocolate can easily overtake that judgment. As I double back to my early childhood impressions, I can see how the euphoria and exuberance of our desires can be blinding. In the case of a new relationship, it may leave us unable to see who a person really is.

During my school-aged years, my mother dated a guy who said all the right things but always did the opposite. He would come around when it was convenient for him, as long as it did not disrupt his daily activities or whatever else he had going on. A gentlemen's handshake did not mean a hill of beans to this guy. Even I could see it. Charismatic but cunning, well-dressed but broken, industrious but frivolous, he was simply not a man of his word. These descriptions are facts based on his cleverness and the soft skills he deployed in his everyday life. To show deference to the man himself and not use his real name, we will call him Elliot.

What I outlined about Elliot comes not from a judgmental perspective but rather the simple facts as I observed them. In no way did I ever disrespect Elliot. My mother would not have any of that. She loved the man, so I always held my opinion of him to myself. Learning to withhold judgment early in my childhood would prove to be lifesaving some years later, just as Elliot would save me from spending twenty plus years in prison, if not more. More on this later.

Dharius Daniels says it best in his book *Relational Intelligence*: "The Scriptures communicate that because only God knows the circumstances and situations people are wrestling with and sorting through, only God is in the position to make the kind of judgments that render a verdict about a person's future or destiny."[2] Withholding judgment is a hint of wisdom. The fallacy of doing otherwise becomes preparation for the inevitability of oneself being stung by the harsh verdict of another person.

My mother and Elliot had a tumultuous relationship, yet they were joined by their offspring in that of a baby girl. As Elliot proved himself to be unreliable and callous, my mother became hardened by her experiences. As such, she ruled her house with an iron fist. I don't know if or how my mother counted the cost in furthering her relationship with Elliot. Even so, her wisdom and desire in doing so were in stark conflict.

Now, as a young person, I had a strong personality with a boatload of stubbornness. Oftentimes, my desires and decision making did not align with my mother's, and we would clash. This was very much unwise on my part because she usually got the last word one way or the other.

My mother was a fierce woman, taking no prisoners when anyone crossed her. In our community, she was known for always carrying her 357 revolver in her purse (which was never too far away) and not being afraid to use it. No one wanted to be on the other end of the pistol whipping that could occur at any time. The other mothers were just as fierce, and they all respected each other's space. If the kids got into fist fights, they would make us finish what was started. There was no coming back to mommy looking for sympathy. You owned whatever mess you made of any youthful relationships gone bad.

As we grow older, each of us will undoubtedly make consequential decisions that will call our judgment into question. At times, we might push too hard to achieve our desires, leaving patience and good judgment at the door. So often, this impatience sets the stage for massive discontentment and heartache. We must master the art of managing our desires alongside that which we know to be unwise. Not to be too ominous here, but even though it is hard to do, we must—lest we become what we loathe.

I am simply saying that good judgment is a vital character trait, and when our good judgment is compromised by our own unhealthy desires—the results of which could be ruinous—we can lean on God's hands of grace to carry us through.

Mama was a single mother with now two children and the instinct to protect her offspring at any cost. And she did just that. Before my sister was born, I had no problems being the only child. However, if there were to be a sibling, I had hoped it would be another boy—a rough rider to join me in navigating public housing. Welcoming a baby sister was a surprising highlight and a joyous occasion.

As the years moved along, my sister and I did not have much of a relationship. I was protective of her, but at five years apart, we did not have very much in common. She had her friends and I had mine. She liked certain foods that I did not, and vice versa, and we had notably different personalities. In certain instances, I could see my sister's personality echoing my mother's. They both loved the notion of having a good time, enjoyed having lots of people around, and enjoyed the smell and taste of good Cajun food.

My mother also loved a clean house. Either she would clean or she'd have a friend or relative help her clean while we played outside. The windows would be thrown wide open with Teddy Pendergrass or some other artist playing in the background while she encased the floors with Pine Sol. Walking into a clean apartment with the smell of cleaner solution tickling my nostrils brought a smile to my face every time. Just after cleaning, there would be some dish on the stove. My mom loved cooking. Her spaghetti with a ton of meat comes to mind, including chicken wings, Italian sausage, ground beef, and shrimp. Basically, more meat than spaghetti and sauce. My sister eventually joined my mother in loving to make good food in a clean house.

I was content. Even with very little exposure to a world outside of public housing at this point. Juxtaposed against my mother and sister, I enjoyed good competition (basketball, in particular) and loathed the idea of having lots of people around. I was always careful to limit my surroundings, as to not include people I did not know well. A guardsman and somewhat of a militaristic being, I had no problem enjoying my own company.

Whilst I learned to appreciate the little we had, I nonetheless felt the plight of it all, and it drove me to be a hard worker throughout my life. Increasingly, my mother struggled to make her dollars stretch, though she took them as far as possible. I remember the stigma of being on food stamps and welfare. Still, my mother held her head high, undaunted by her circumstances. It had simply been the cost of loving love.

My mother wanted to be in a loving and safe relationship, but as many times as she tried—at least as far as I could tell— the risk for her far outweighed the benefits. To that point, I had not witnessed my mother being truly loved by or cared for by a man. This played a part in developing my worldview as it related to male and female relationships. Consequently, I eventually made some big mistakes in how I engaged with girls and, later in life, women.

At the same time, my zeal to shelter the opposite sex could be uncompromising. There is a thin line between covering and controlling, but the difference is very much distinct.

Covering is sheltering from harm and stress; controlling, I believe, is a heavy hand of forceful directives attached to consequences. Whilst I never assigned consequences in my relationships, I was uncompromising and firm in my positions. As I grew older, I learned to be more flexible and accepting of the fact that there just may be a better way to provide a loving cover. As men, we must err on the side of covering so that it can never be misconstrued for control.

Because my mother loved having lots of people around, there were people in our apartment all the time. Most likely, this was an effort to mask the pain of relationships gone bad. Still, all sorts of people enjoyed my mother's hospitality. Occasionally, a few of them would bring their own bottle of whatever they were drinking. Others would partake of whatever she had in stock.

I do not recall getting chastised a lot by my mother, but when it did occur, it was a big deal—no matter who was around. My stubborn reaction to my mother's wielding of the rod was indeed a showdown. Most often, for me, crying was not an option—and she, being the disciplinarian that she was, would keep going until she saw a tear. If I did not feel like playing the "who will break first" game, I would shed a tear quickly so I could get on to whatever I was doing.

Genuinely speaking, I was never phased by her antics. I suppose I understood well, even at a young age, that she was doing it all single handedly, and I was very much indifferent to her stages and moods.

Then again, as I said previously, she always referred to me as the most indifferent person she knew. As might be expected of a stubborn child, I did not care that she said this. It did not bother me in the least bit—and I suppose that irritated the heck out of her, too. I simply had my own way of processing and thinking about things, never beholden to the thoughts and ideas of others.

Because my biological pops lived in another state, we had limited-to-no daily connection during these years. His focus, rightly so, was on his family in Texas. From time to time, I would visit him during the summertime. Our worlds were so different that I simply did not understand him and he did not understand me. One common trait, though, was that we both were hot tempered. Maybe his was because he was under immense pressure, whatever that could have been. Perhaps mine was that I was living under meager circumstances back in Baton Rouge. In any case, although I was only eleven or so years old, I had already learned that the cost of love was too high a price for me to pay.

I had not seen the true reciprocity of love between a boy and his father or a man and his son. As a result, I would go on to make the transition from boyhood to manhood not from real-life application or after seeing it modeled in a consistent way, but rather from how I imagined a man should move and conduct himself. Men of character must be involved in the lives of young boys. Men in our communities must cement themselves as fathers, mentors, sponsors, and counselors, without being insistent or pushy.

At the time, if anyone came across as high and mighty or overbearing, I would immediately disconnect, quickly and angrily. I did not like forceful directives. When I eventually had boys of my own, I had to learn to intentionally and consistently drop nuggets of rationality on them and then move on. They may not have accepted it right then; however, I knew they would eventually recall and deploy those nuggets of rationality when they needed them.

Sometimes, just seeing true manhood modeled is enough. If we can see it, we can be it.

Food stamps back then were notably different than paper dollar green currency, and taking them into the grocery store could be embarrassing. Then there was that thick block of cheese, at free or reduced cost, that we would have to stand in line to take home. I have to say, it made for some good macaroni and cheese. I ate so much of this dish that I would run from macaroni and cheese later in life.

So many humiliating moments and situations happened throughout childhood, as happen to us all: Wearing shoes from "Payless" shoe store (a deep discount store) was almost comparable to walking barefoot. Riding in cars that the kids made fun of. Standing in front of the class to give a speech or presentation and forgetting lines. Slipping and falling only to hear laughter. Failing to make the school athletics team. Being cheated on by your little girlfriend or boyfriend. We will not all identify with each one of the examples listed, but the point is that variations on these moments happen to us all. I have come to learn that one of the primary reasons we feel the sting of an embarrassing or humiliating moment is because we care a bit too much about how we are perceived or what others think.

Even as an "indifferent" child, as mama pointed out, I felt it too. I wonder if the difference is that I had no influence over certain embarrassing moments, versus the grace I quickly gave myself after an embarrassing moment that was under my control. My indifferent nature does allow me to recover quickly. At the same time, individuals that would criticize, judge, or laugh at the pain of another person were probably not the company to keep.

At a very early age, I was very good about placing distance between me and anyone I felt did not mean me any good. I developed the gift of goodbye, or easily distancing myself. If my personality did not jive with someone else's, it was no problem for me to move on. However, for me to move on from any relationship, I had to have heard with my own ears or seen with my own eyes an action that could give me cause to pause. I was a fierce protector of my young friends. Life was teaching me to love people where they are, given that time and chance happens to us all.

Do what you say you will do; no excuses.

There was an amusement park called Fun Fair Park on Airline Highway in Baton Rouge. Basically, a small-scale Six Flags. All the kids loved going there. This was around the age of eleven—which I remember ever so clearly, as it was when breakdancing was gaining popularity. Who among us kids at the time questioned whether we could take an old cardboard box from the local corner store, split it in two, and start spinning on our backs? Oh, and I cannot forget about the boombox I had gotten one Christmas to embellish our pop-locking dance moves.

Well, Elliot being Elliot had promised my sister and I that he would bring us to Fun Fair Park. Holding staunchly to Elliot's word, my mother made sure we were dressed and ready to go on Elliot's arrival. Minutes ticked away, which led to hours ticking away, then nightfall—no Elliot. No calls from Elliot. Nothing. He had made promises that, I reasoned, he was not intending to keep. It was that, or he had totally forgotten about my sister (his biological daughter) and I.

The next day, I was faced with the humiliation of sharing with my friends that I had not gone to Fun Fair Park as I had told them all I would. So, what happened—why didn't you go? Ah, I knew you were lying about going to Fun Fair Park. Yeah, you would have been lucky if you did go. Humiliated but in control of my reaction, I took the taunting and kept it moving. I suppose I noticed that it was not like these kids frequented Fun Fair Park often either, and perhaps, they were living vicariously through any of us who had the chance to go.

I was also learning quickly that the commitments that come out of one's mouth must be kept. No excuses!

By now, I had sized Elliot up and deeply understood the character of the man. A smooth-talking ladies' man, well-dressed, and a partier, this guy could sell you a lifeboat in the desert. I knew enough to know that I had to keep him at a distance. I had been crushed enough by his inability to keep his commitments. My mother, on the other hand, held on to all his shenanigans and commitments even though she also knew he would not follow through. She simply loved the man.

In my mind, a man's word was much more valuable than his money or any other tangible possessions. Doing what you say you will do means honoring your commitments. Outside of my mother, I had never seen anyone consistently honor their commitments—not friends, not acquaintances, not even family members. I had one of two pathways to take: follow everyone else and evade or neglect to fill my commitments, or become known as the person who delivers. Whilst choosing the latter is an ordinary act, consistently delivering on commitments can be extraordinary. Some may describe this as rigid; I see it as distinguished. The quaint view of a distinguished gentleman who commands respect by monitoring what comes out of his mouth and keeping his commitments.

"Thank God it ain't no worse." Those words often rang from the lips of my mother. From what I could gather, there was a certain sentiment of inner peace communicated when my elders used those words. I surmised that they understood there would always be problems, challenges, and disappointments, but with a balanced perspective that troubles don't always last. There would also be some good from the ebbs and flows of life. Thank God it ain't no worse—because it certainly could always be worse.

When tough times are placed in our path, whether or not they were the result of our decisions, we must walk through them, recognizing that the sun will still rise the next day. When it does, we will have another opportunity to make it through to the other side of the issue. If we give in or give up too soon, we miss the opportunity to see that brighter day.

That brighter day could be filled with trusted friends, a good movie, releasing energy with some good exercise, reading a good book, traveling to a favorite destination, dining at a favorite food spot, or whatever it is that brings a smile. There is always something to be thankful for. There will be right turns and left turns, ups and downs—even moving in a circular motion at times—but a bit of thankfulness in those moments is nothing short of miraculous.

When issues and storms have come my way, as a child and even as an adult, watching a good television show or movie has always been my relaxation method of choice. During those stages of childhood when I had gotten into some sort of trouble, or even when my mother had her music going with her friends visiting, you could find me in a room watching a television show or movie. It took my mind away from my troubles, a mental escape to keep me from rehashing the issue over and over again. I suppose my very own three-step path back to gratitude entailed taking time to reflect on the issue or storm, taking time for a mental break, and then taking time to determine my next steps and pivot. Even now, and whilst it is difficult, I am still practicing being thankful in the midst of the issues and storms that come my way every day.

My mother worked in both private security at stores and, at a certain point, as a certified nursing assistant at the homes of wealthy people. With a strong work ethic and the ability to connect with her patients, she was always lauded with appreciation. She would come home with small trin-kets and gifts they had given her, only to give them to me or others. They entrusted her with their cars and their homes, and she enjoyed the accruements of verbal affirmation and tangible gifts. One of those wealthy individuals, I will never forget, was Mr. Kantrow. He was my mother's favorite person to take care of at the time, and my mother was his favorite home-care provider. I still have the silver-banded Timex self-wind watch he gave to my mother, who in turn gave it to me.

For reasons I cannot explain, I held on to it then and still have it now.

The reciprocity of thankfulness between my mother and her patients was on full display. I think my mother was appreciative of being needed by individuals who appreciated her efforts. In many cases, those efforts went beyond what the job required. Most of the time, when the patients' families did not or would not visit them, my mother stepped in as their family to fill that void. This sometimes entailed driving patients around for hours in the day to take their mind off their lack of familial presence and support. She took patients shopping or to their favorite dining places (most of the time, good Cajun food), then sat with them for hours talking and laughing. When her patients would get sick and need to be admitted to the hospital, there went my mother, visiting them in the hospital outside of her normal working hours—all in an effort to keep their minds off their troubles.

They were thankful for her caregiving skills and bedside manners, and she was thankful for the opportunity to earn money and provide essential human care. When the patients' behavior was rude or based in racist comments, she did not take it personally. She did, however, correct such behavior in her own novel—and characteristically stern—ways. As I watched from afar, though never too far away, I appreciated these visible, noncommunicative life lessons. She left an indelible mark on all the people she cared for, and this gave me a window into the soul of the woman and her respect for humankind.

Exposure to issues and storms is inevitable. Think about being literally caught up in a storm, such as a tornado or hurricane, with violent rotating or driving winds. Having been caught up in my share of hurricanes, I can say that there is panic, commotion, anxiety, lack of foresight—the storm terrorizes the community and rips through your residence, leaving a trail of destruction in its path. Such as the case with issues and storms in our lives.

As children, we have very little control over the storms that we're exposed to. Later on in life, some of those experiences come from our very own life choices, self-inflicted, with no one to blame but ourselves. The challenge is, who likes that level of self-reflection? It is much easier to deflect, evading that person in the mirror. We can use our life experiences, issues, and storms to fan flames of bitterness, hatred, and vengeance, but in the end, this will only compromise our own stability and mental health. We will miss out on all the gifts that life can bring.

To face our issues and storms with a bit of thankfulness? It is difficult to do, but extraordinary. That is when we become fully functioning human beings—like my mother and the elders who influenced my childhood. Walking testimonies touching the lives of others. Ordinary people demonstrating the extraordinary gift of giving thanks in all things.

Being thankful in the midst of a storm is not a natural human action. Even so, practice drives progress. And at any rate, we can always thank God it ain't no worse.

LEVELING UP

To move people to your side, you need to make them care. You will need your facts, your figures, your argument to be rock solid. But you will also need an approach that goes back millennia: You must appeal to people's hearts, not just their heads.[3]

"Ms. Gail, you have been a staple in these here apartments. I just want you to know that there will be two young men who will make it out—and one is your son Carnell." My mother shared these words with me almost two decades ago, having come from the gentleman who managed and who eventually owned the Suburban apartments. How did he know? What did he see? It must have been Providence in the projects, as his proclamation was nearly 100 percent accurate.

The only models of success I saw as a pre-teen were professional athletes and entertainers. I had not been exposed to engineers, lawyers, doctors, CEOs, investment bankers, etc. For that matter, I had not been exposed to successful entrepreneurial tradesmen, either. Even so, I could look at my environment and know what I did not want out of life. Hence, early on, the only dream I could imagine was to be a professional basketball player.

Call it God-given prudence, but I could see, adjust, and pivot my actions from an early age. I did not necessarily have to touch fire to know that it was hot. Observing others' plights was enough for me. See better, know better, and do better. On the other side of the spectrum, I had always dreamed of more. Even with little exposure to "more," I knew it had to exist. At the time, my sophomoric thinking believed it meant more money, more house, more clothes, more food.

After acquiring more, it is then a matter of being judicious with what you have. The problem comes in when acquisition crosses the line into greed, which then can lend itself to attaining more by any means necessary—legal or illegal. I have often said that an ambitious, desperate person is a dangerous person, but an ambitious and disciplined person is a prolific person. In that regard, ambition is a necessary ingredient for personal fulfillment. I knew enough at the time to understand that I did not want to acquire more in the way I had seen others pilfer or cheat to do. I also credit my mother. Watching her struggling and working diligently for what she wanted and not taking the easy way out made it easier for me to make the right decisions.

My mother's work ethic was an inspiration to me. She didn't know, but I was always watching and taking mental notes. In the last days of her life, she was still trying to work and take care of her patients from her very own hospital bed as she was slowly slipping away into eternity. She left such a deep-rooted impression on my view of hard work. I love her all the more for it.

As we set goals and dreams, we often overlook the value of the journey itself. My life's path eventually wound through the incredible world of corporate America, and the company where I worked was extremely safety conscious. It employed a "journey management plan" any time employees traveled on behalf of the company. It would outline the demands of the trip, as well as the methods and passages you would take to get to a destination safely. It would include such things as the reason for the trip, confirming whether you are traveling with any other colleagues, the drivers and passengers, dates and times of arrivals and departures, the route to be taken, and any known hazards. The journey toward our own dreams and hopes should be no less protected. We need to be clear, specific, and diligent about the pursuit of our ambitions, setting goals that are as thorough as a personal journey management plan.

Over the years and with God's hand, I came to accumulate more than I had imagined possible. I learned that acquiring more and wanting more is not a bad thing. In fact, just the opposite. I now understand that it is the hand of God that allows for more. To be clear, whilst we may ask for and strive for what we want, it does not mean God will act with immediacy. It may not be His time to provide more; even so, we must be diligent in seeking His hand. To dream and to hope is to journey towards the mark of manifestation. Enjoy the ride along the way, but whatever you do, do not come to a complete stop. Keep the mark in play, no matter how long it takes.

*Commitment to greatness does not care
about circumstance; make the best use of
what you have to achieve what you want.*

Both Magic Johnson and Larry Bird were phenomenal basketball players in the late 1970s, whilst still playing for their respective universities. They finally joined the National Basketball Association (NBA) in the late 1970s and became fierce competitors throughout the early 1980s. By 1984, in the early stages of their NBA careers, I had reached the tender age of thirteen, with sports (and basketball in particular) becoming my pastime of choice. In middle school, I was known for my pure and raw athletic talent—with wicked speed, better-than-average basketball handling, and a decent mid-range jump shot.

No one could not tell me I was not going to be the next Magic Johnson.

Since I was tall, lean, and fast for my age, I also ran track for the middle school athletic program. Sporting competitions at that level came easy. I piled up a number of the round, blue, embroidered badges from the Presidential Physical Fitness Awards. These were badges of honor indicating to me that the raw talent I relied upon—more so than a diligent work ethic— was enough to make me one of the best athletes at my middle school. I did not realize at the time that raw talent was just not enough for greatness. At least, not at the Magic Johnson and Larry Bird levels. The passion for basketball was there, but I lacked the deep level of consistent commitment to be great.

On the other side of the coin, playing basketball in public housing was a bit different than playing organized basketball at school. In public housing, you had to be good enough to get picked to play, even if you were playing with the bigger kids. I was always picked to play and did not like to lose. You could say I was a fierce competitor amongst the kids my age.

The basketball court was in the middle of the apartments, with enough cement for full court action. Some of the residents could walk outside their sliding back doors and there it was—a large, open area for basketball and other sports, making the most out of the space with anything we could think of. Just about twenty feet from the basketball court was the washeteria. Sometimes the machines worked; most of the time, they did not. Usually, the kids had to help our mothers haul loads of clothes to a nearby, more reliable washeteria. Similarly, there sometimes were two functioning goals for full-court play, and sometimes (more than half the time) we could only play half-court.

On one side of the basketball court, there was just enough space to play tackle football—without any pads, of course. The best way to describe football in that apartment complex would be to think of rugby with American football rules. It was physical, brutal, filled with trash talk, and great. It was always a treat to see the older, bigger kids play. Some of them were multi-talented stars of several sports. Tim, for example, was incredible to watch on the football "field given his fearlessness and physicality." He was also a left hander who had mad basketball handles and could pull up for a jump shot anywhere on the court. Most times, it was lights out—which meant he was sure to make the shot. A scoring phenomenon. Even with the basketball goal tilted or uneven, scoring buckets was no problem for many of us, especially Tim. The name of the game was making the best use of what was available.

I played basketball so much that I was bound to break something, almost as a matter of course. Coming off a screen on the right side, preparing to receive the ball from one of my teammates and shoot a mid-range jumper, I took my eye off the ball before fully catching it, and the ball crushed my finger. I rushed to our apartment, which at the time was in the back of the complex and in the corner and not far from where the basketball courts were. Number 143. A small three-bedroom apartment—the one that my mother worked so hard to keep clean. Not for the first time, my mother met me at the door, assessed the damage, and took me to Earl K. Long Hospital to get checked out. This time, culminating in a cast for my broken finger.

Earl K. Long Hospital was approximately ten miles from the apartment complex, just off Airline Highway. I did not like going to this hospital. It was always full. You could expect to spend all day or all night there before finally being seen by any hospital personnel. However, I could at least appreciate that it was the only option. I knew this hospital well. It's where I went for required and routine vaccinations, which I did not like in the first place. It did not help one bit that we would be there literally all day for a simple vaccination. From time to time, I also suffered with aching legs, mostly during the middle of the night, requiring medical attention. And then there were the injuries.

Earl K. Long—yep, that same charitable hospital where I was born—was the hospital that everyone from public housing frequented. Whilst use of public or charitable facilities is a necessity for many people, it does not have to be the totality of our life's story. The conundrum of a life spent working hard and yet still being at or below the poverty line is a hard pill to swallow. At the same time, running a business while managing labor costs to stay in business is a hard balancing act as well. It's not so easy to just work multiple jobs, as many claim to be the solution, especially since many individuals have children to care for at the same time as this struggle. It's also not so easy to say, "just raise wages," which then puts a strain on operations that could lead to downsizing or going out of business. There are no easy answers to complex issues, but the commitment to aspire to a better place and space in spite of the complexity can be rewarded in time.

*The foundation of unity and brotherhood
sits at the crux of trust and loyalty.*

As soon as the cast was off, I was back on the basketball court with the other kids, talking trash and draining shots with the best of them. Trash talking was the *best.*

You can't hold me.

Lights out—come back tomorrow.

Mama, come get your son—he's done.

Bottom of the net—game over, son.

Next.

Once your team lost, it could be hours before you got back on the court. Several kids were already waiting with "next up," and they could pick anyone that was not playing to be on their team. If you were not any good, you literally did not have a chance to play. To that end, the smaller kids—that is, the kids that were even younger than me—mostly played in the late evenings once the bigger kids had moved on.

Many of the kids, both young and old, had the same rules my mother had for me: be sure to be back in the apartment before the street lights came on. I would surmise this meant, at least from my mother's perspective, that there was too much going on once night fell. I always felt clever staying out a bit later whenever she was not home. The street lights would illuminate, and I would still be huddled up with my friends or playing basketball under the yellow glow, testing the boundaries that my mother had set.

The older kids in my community were so very talented that I know they could have played at the collegiate level. A lot can be said for lack of exposure and the lack of ambition, given that we lacked any real, touchable role models to draw inspiration from. The "streets" had a powerful hold on many of these kids, and they sought to get ahold of money mostly by any means necessary, fighting with each other just because it was inevitable.

One day, when the big yellow bus dropped us off right in front of our big yellow apartments, a ruckus broke out. It was mayhem. The older kids from the apartment complex were locked into a smackdown against the older kids from other parts of the city. Apparently, the trash talk had gone too far at the high school; the kids who lived in other parts of the city decided to drive over and finish it. Fists were flying, elbows and jabs were taken and given, bodies were slammed, faces were bruised. The kids from other parts of the city were looking for just one person in the apartment complex, but when they jumped that kid, all the others jumped to defend. This was the first time in my young life that I had observed loyalty displayed at this level—at least on the physical side of things.

Whilst I dare not compare this type of loyalty to those in the military, I am, however, reminded of the way soldiers speak of defending and protecting their own, and loathing anyone who would disrespect or harm their fellow comrades. One of my favorite pastimes as an adult is reading books and watching movies about the military, immersing myself in their stories of secrecy, stealth, and strength. I have tremendous respect for the kind of trust and loyalty they are able to engender, exuding passion and intensity. The US military is nothing short of exemplary and extraordinary at every branch and every level, and I am appreciative of such sacrificial service.

Simon Sinek once interviewed Navy SEALs about their way of illustrating or expressing trust and loyalty. He asked how this branch of the military selected its members. The response was that it was based on performance and trust—and believe it or not, performance was not ranked the highest on the rating scale. The Navy SEALs are okay with a medium or even low performance if it is also a high-trust person. Trust is the foundation. They stated, "I can trust you with my life but can I trust you with my money and my wife?"[4] The military is a true and demonstrable example of unity and brotherhood, which allows it to be the shining, selfless symbol of greatness.

But there must be reciprocity in both trust and loyalty; otherwise, it becomes exploitation.

Back in the early to mid-1990s, we had green-and-white "scantron sheets" that were used for taking multiple-choice tests and quizzes. Often, the assignment would be to take notes and read handouts in preparation for tests or pop quizzes, then the room full of sixth and seventh graders, fearful of getting a bad grade, would go home and study judiciously. And me? Well, my head and my heart just did not align when it came to studying. School was just not something I enjoyed. My head had done the calculation and knew that if I did not study, I was sure to fail the test or pop quiz. My heart, on the other hand, was not so good at calculations. It said, "You can just 'wing it.' Mark all the same letters on the scantron and there is a 50/50 chance you will pass the test anyway. Probably."

The head is a wonderfully complex aspect of ourselves. It is the center for learning, logic, reasoning, and processing information. When the head takes us through a path of logic and reasoning, it also accounts for the downside of any thoughts and decisions we're exploring. This is to say, the head processes information incredibly fast, with assessments from many different angles.

As for the heart, it contains our innermost nature—our desires, our make-up, and our intuition. It is my position that the heart drives peace or chaos within our souls. When both the head and the heart are aligned when it comes to our thoughts, desires, and decisions, we can only hope that wisdom abounds, making it a challenge to color outside the lines of illegality and destruction. Thus, our wholesome ambitions are center stage and surely attainable. On the other side of that coin, when our head and heart are misaligned, or the heart has seeds of a warring nature contrasting to that of the head, we see the instigation of chaos.

Well, on pop quiz day, all I could do was gawk at the scantron like a deer in headlights. No study, no preparation—stunned, as if the answers were going to pop into my head by osmosis, without any meaningful effort. Interestingly enough, my head knew what needed to be done. It had made calculations about what would happen if I did study; however, my heart just would not follow along. I had no desire to put forth effort and display studiousness. Perhaps I thought I was just too cool to study. After all, I did have a high level of cachet in middle school, and that meant more to me than passing tests and pop quizzes.

This misalignment between my head and my heart led to missed entrepreneurial learning opportunities, too. Before he passed away, my uncle David was the patriarch on my mother's side of the family. He was a young man when I was a teen, just in his thirties but with the heart and soul of an older, wiser man. He was an entrepreneur, an athlete, a husband, and a father, and he loved his entire family. His sisters and brothers held him in the highest esteem, and he had several nephews, including me, that he wanted to spend time with to teach us about business, among other things. He encouraged me and

my other cousins to join him in working at the window cleaning business that he owned.

I did join him on a few occasions, but I only half paid any
attention. My head knew that if I had made the effort to join
him consistently, I would learn how entrepreneurial business
is conducted, even at my young age. But no, not me. My heart
just was not in it. It was miles away, and the whole time I was
longing to play basketball with friends.

Remember that relative that I mentioned earlier? The one
who lived in a small town in Louisiana and I accompanied to
North Carolina because of his fear of flying? Well, this same
relative spent hours and hours with my uncle, learning how
entrepreneurship was done. And yes, this is the same relative
who has earned a small fortune in the entrepreneurship space.

*The brilliance of paying attention
to the head and the heart: insight
from two titans in their own right.*

Eleanor Roosevelt once said, "To handle yourself, use your head; to handle others, use your heart." ER, as she was often called, had a difficult upbringing and, later, a rather difficult marriage to Franklin Roosevelt. There is some documentation to suggest that ER and Franklin were even distant cousins and that several family members did not want them to marry. Against the naysayers, they wed anyway, though it ultimately became a marriage of convenience and a political partnership. ER had a tumultuous relationship with her mother-in-law, who was said to be very controlling. She had children, though there are reports that she did not want children and thought she was ill-suited to parent them. During the marriage, ER discovered Franklin had an affair; subsequently, Franklin was stricken with a paralytic illness. Nevertheless, ER remained by his side.

Over the years, ER increasingly became a political powerhouse, making several controversial decisions. One of those controversial decisions was to not support her cousin Theodore for governor of New York, but rather openly supported his opponent. ER was known to be quite liberal and a fierce advocate and activist. She advocated in support of the expanded roles of women in the workplace and supported the civil rights of African Americans and Asian Americans during a time when this proved to be against the establishment.[5]

I cannot help but ponder how she made her decisions. Did she often have an aligned head and heart? Did she lead with her heart? Did her head factor into the consequences of her decisions? When she chose to stay married after the discovery of the affair, were both her head and heart aligned?

However the calculation was made, one must imagine her counting the cost of her decisions to herself and yet still making a profound impact on humankind. Whilst both ER and Franklin decided to stay married, by all means keeping their own agendas, ER became one of the most admired women in the world. Had any other decisions been made, one could only hope that her impact would have been just the same.

"A good head and a good heart are always a formidable combination, but when you add to that a literate tongue or pen, then you have something very special." Nelson Mandela, a formidable leader in his own right, said these words. Well-educated, well-spoken, charismatic, and a lawyer by trade, Mandela disrupted the status quo in South Africa.

Whilst he made some missteps and miscalculations in going about the business of pursuing equal justice, the world over watched Nelson Mandela bravely take on the brutal apartheid regime that terrorized its own people. At the time, Black folks in South Africa could not travel to certain places or do certain things within the country, and Mandela did not stand for it. There came a decision-making point where Nelson Mandela evolved and developed a philosophy of fighting against apartheid with the notion of matching force with equal force. Eventually, he had run-ins with the South African government and its policies, ultimately landing him a life sentence in prison.[6]

After spending more than twenty-seven years in prison, Nelson Mandela was released at the age of seventy-two. Just four years removed from prison, he became the president of the same country where he, at one point, could not even own real estate. A sagacious statesman, Nelson Mandela did not lament the hardship of imprisonment, but rather illuminated the novel concept of equal justice under law and ultimately won a Nobel Prize for his demonstration of peace and reconciliation. With the thousands of decisions made by Nelson Mandela, I would surmise that his head and his heart were at times at war with each other. Notwithstanding, intelligence and an aura of unforgettable presence radiated from the man, making him a formidable champion for good.

Among the sheer volume of decisions we make each day, a plethora of them will impact people, in good and bad ways. Even at a young age, our decisions define who we are and the character we possess. Our upbringing, including the environment we're in, plays a critical role at how we process and make those decisions. It's worth examining whether our experiences drive a hard heart and a disillusioned head or make provision for an altruistic heart and a judicious head. Do we learn to paralyze ourselves when making decisions, our heads becoming hardwired to overthink and seized by procrastination? These are just a few of the complexities inherent in the alignment of our head and our heart.

Who knows and understands the heart? It has a mind of its own. Be diligent in the guardship of the heart; it must be handled with providential care. "The heart steers the head. And if it's heart versus head, I promise you, pure logic is losing nine times out of ten."[7] Eleanor Roosevelt and Nelson Mandela were very much aware of the dichotomy that exists between the head and the heart. We must take time to listen to both.

*It takes courage to defend
and protect what is right.*

My head and my heart have always been aligned when it comes to people being misused or abused. If my mother was ever in the middle of some sort of altercation, there I would find myself, right by her side or stepping in the middle in some subtle way. The same went for my young friends Chris or Dante or others—I always found myself right by their side, helping to resolve things either directly or indirectly. My head would process and make calculations of the psychological impact of the abuse, and my heart would follow with my own human nature as a protector and defender. This, I believe, is one of the reasons I garnered that cachet at middle school. It was rare that the other kids would mistreat anyone close to me or my posse, as it were. But that cachet didn't always show up in a good way.

One early morning, before the start of class, there was an altercation involving one of my friends and another kid. I jumped in the middle, defending my friend, and told the other kid that we all would finish this beef at recess. This kid, probably making his calculations of what was to come during recess, did not wait for recess. Shortly after I turned to walk away—*wham!* A sucker punch to the back of the head. I never saw it coming. For a brief period, I did not remember anything or anyone. It felt like I had been hit with a brick. I was slow to get up, but as soon as I was able to gather myself, instinctively, I jumped back up to finish what was started—this time, face to face. Only, instead of settling the matter my way, the teacher intervened, separated us, and threatened suspension.

From this experience, I picked up the habit of closely studying anyone who would take an adversarial position during a dispute or exchange of unfriendly words. I started to keenly watch mannerisms, facial expressions, movement, and posture, avoiding turning my back to tense or contentious situations as much as I possibly could. I became hypersensitive, even conscious enough to avoid sitting with my back to any exit or entrance. The thought of that sucker punch was an ever-present reminder to me of the speed at which a situation can become unstable.

The beauty of experience is that, if we take the lesson, we do not have to repeat the lesson. Over the years, my vigilance evolved from direct or physical involvement into a development of diplomacy. I learned the power of words. I learned to be slow to speak and quick to listen. I became stoic and stealthy in my thoughts and responses. When folks would come to me in times of trouble, I would give my head and my heart time to process and find the right words. Not one to bask in neither the misfortune nor the misgivings of anyone, I was very much a young man with an old man's spirit. On those rare occasions when my pops would come to visit Louisiana from Texas, my great uncle would see us coming and jokingly say to me, "What's up, old man—where's your son?"

During my younger teen years, I started visiting my aunts and my grandmother on my pop's side of the family. My aunt, one of the matriarchs in the family, was gracious, smooth, thoughtful, and welcoming. I spent a great deal of time with her and her family. When they took me in, it was a whole world away from public housing. She, her husband, and kids were a complete, intact family, with a beautiful and well-kept home. This was perhaps my first exposure to what the true nucleus of a family should look like. It was an inspiration to me. Similarly, my grandmother and grandfather had a home with plenty of land for all the grandkids to run around and play in. On those rare occasions when I would visit, I remember my grandfather would always bless me with a few quarters. He did not have much, yet he gave anyway.

These visits instilled in me a love for land and cattle, which stayed with me the rest of my life. Later on, I would eventually buy acres of land and develop a ranch-style habitat alongside one of my uncles. Exposure to the very idea of land and cattle—there is that word again, "exposure"—gave me access to a world outside of public housing.

Here, I want to note that while my mother had a great command of the expletives portion of the English language, she never disparaged my pops, nor my sister's pops, nor anyone else for any lack of support she felt, financial or otherwise. Not that I can remember. Whilst my mother had a soft spot for her family members outside of my sister and I, she managed her relationships with family members using both her head and her heart judiciously—ever mindful of the chaos that can so easily plague a family.

When times were tight, my mother always found a way to earn money for our school clothes and other necessities. No excuses. Every day after school, she would tell us to "Take off those school clothes" as we could not afford to get them dirty. We were sure to wear them again soon, if not in the same week, then in the following. And these were the days when it was a whole "thing" to have your jeans starched and crisp to the point that they could almost stand on their own. If you had one wrinkle in sight, you were sure to be teased. We would always have a couple of cans of starch and a broken-down ironing board tucked away in a corner somewhere in the house because there was no chance we were going to some dry-cleaning place to have it done. There was no extra money for that. My mother ironed and pressed everything. She ironed and pressed her uniforms, ironed and pressed our clothes—and after watching and learning from her, I took over that chore and became meticulous about ironing my jeans.

Aside from my mother's occasional shenanigans, I have always held a profound respect for her. Her sacrifice and loyalty to her children, her family, and her friends were a marvel to witness. Oh, and by the way, she was a comedic genius, too. The woman had all *kinds* of jokes. Before you left her presence, you were sure to be bent over in stitches, laughing uncontrollably. My mother had all sorts of decisions to make, and she did not always get the balance of the head and heart right. Most of the time, she led with the heart, forgetting that her head had to be a part of all her decision making.

As a person who is extremely logical and practical by nature, I did not always make enough space for the heart to play its role. My primary and sometimes sole decision-making apparatus was my head. Over the years, I made some decisions that were colossal wins and some that were colossal failures. Even now, I must challenge myself on big decisions to ensure I find that balance. Often, I turn to trustworthy people who make decisions by leading with their hearts, to test my concepts or any big decisions I need to make personally. Otherwise, most of my decisions would likely be led by the head only.

On the other side of that coin, leading with the heart and leaving little space for the head to play a role in decisions can leave a person to be taken advantage of or to become the aggressor and take advantage of someone else. If you are someone that often makes decisions with the heart first, consider including people in your circle who you trust and who lead with the head, to bring balance and counsel through the added dimension of reason and logic. I consciously do this to challenge my nature, and I invite you to do it as well.

The goal is to be able to see the whole board, or as much of the board as possible, when making big decisions. A trusted circle of wise counsel can help keep each of us balanced.

Before I was baptized at the age of fifteen, there were signals and signs of God existing throughout my formative years. However, I had not yet fully internalized that an encounter with God is a life-changing event. Mostly, my mother would take my sister and I to church on holidays and special occasions, and this was the extent of my exposure. I saw God's love from the inside of God's house, not realizing that God's love is what kept my mother, my sister, and me from drowning in the waters of life— that my mother was simply treading long enough to see the Glory of the water whilst managing to keep her head above it.

With neither a swimming pool nor a beach nearby, I hadn't yet learned how to swim for real, but when it came to the waters of my very existence, I was following my mother's example and learning to tread just as she did. And she was the absolute best at it—protecting, providing, and making those ends meet as a single parent despite the unpredictability of the waves of challenges that rolled in, one right after the other. We may have been at or just over the poverty line, but I can emphatically say that my sister and I never missed a meal, we were clothed with the best low-cost clothing money could buy, and our small three-bedroom apartment was just enough for the three of us. The meals and clothes may not have been what we wanted on every occasion, but our bellies were cared for and our clothes were clean, fitted, and pressed. I had seen enough to know that this was a remarkable effort by my mother. And with relatives, friends, and others moving in and out of jail or prison, I was just clever enough to know that God's hand was on my life as I continued to dodge the ruinous impacts of getting into any major trouble. The waters weren't always calm, but neither had they overtaken us.

I must pause here to say that God gave each of us the freedom of choice, to make our own decisions in all their various forms. I take this pause because, at the time, I could not process seeing people impacted by hardships and challenges. Yet, we have to be mindful that sometimes hardships and challenges come from our very own actions, or perhaps from the actions of our own ancestral family. This is to say that even the choices and decisions that appear to be mundane are actually critical—and this is when we must be careful in how we approach the sovereignty of God. When we think we have been good or have done good, yet bad things happen, it's easy to have a skewed perspective of God. However, hardships and challenges are ever present. Whilst taking ownership for our decisions in those circumstances is difficult, especially when those decisions turn out to have undesirable outcomes, the best thing to do is to pray for grace and mercy over all the decisions we make, seeking God's compassion rather than going at it alone. You stand a better chance to manage these things gracefully when God is part of the equation and decides to move one way or the other within it.

This degree of self-reflection is a key ingredient for growth and humility. One of my first experiences in such humility came with the decision of my mother to hold me back a year in elementary school. This was not a direct decision made by me—and it felt like a ton of bricks caved in on me when it happened—but it turned out to be the right decision for me. I know now that I was just not at the level I needed to progress. What felt like a crack in my armor of confidence at the time allowed me to catch up to and then surpass my lagging growth and development. My mother perhaps thought that I would benefit from the redo, forming a more solid educational foundation even as my peers moved on. She thought that if I could start strong, I would finish strong. And I did—with multiple degrees. At the same time, I also realize that, had I consistently made the proper decision to study and do my homework, my mother would not have had to make such a difficult decision for me.

No one wants bad things to happen, especially when those bad things impact us at the hands of someone else. Petition for grace in all decisions, knowing that we do not always make the right ones, and persevere to see the outcome. That hand of grace just might lead to a beautiful outcome that lifts you up and impacts the generations behind you in some unforeseen way.

*At the center of change is progression,
regression, or perhaps aggression—
the beauty is, you get to decide.*

Envision you or your significant other have worked a job—it does not matter whether it is a white-collar or blue-collar job—where the senior leadership suggests or requests that you move outside of your current state or city and to take a role in another state or city. You have resided in your current state for a very long time, long enough to build a community of friends in your neighborhood, at your church, and through various kid-related activities. You have gotten accustomed to when and where you buy groceries, get your car repaired, and meet friends for happy hour. You are deeply rooted in your way of life. But now you have a decision to make: Do you take the job and give up your life as you know it, or do you resign and give up your accumulated years of service?

You consider starting from scratch, both building a new community and adjusting to new leaders and managers. You also consider the impact on the kids. How will they adjust? Will it be easy for them to make new friends? What will the support structure look like when there is a need? Oh, and then there's the talk with your significant other, who may or may not want to relocate—potentially leaving behind their parents and maybe even close siblings. Relocating is no small decision, by a stretch.

For those of us who enjoy sports, perhaps I can bring this relocation scenario closer to home: What comes to mind when you hear about your favorite athlete getting traded to another team? Professional sports is a business just as much as it is entertainment. That means your favorite player goes through the emotions of having to move to a new city, just as I described a professional relocation. They may have a tumultuous start, but we often forget that they are adjusting to their new teammates, a new coaching style, and the unpredictable nature of reception of the fans. That athlete may very well get off to a great start helping the team to win as intended, but they can also go the other way, putting up disappointing stats, being in contention with the coaching staff, failing to win, and potentially even calling their new contract into question.

In 1986, at fifteen years old, I experienced all of the above during my relocation from Louisiana to Texas. All of the aforementioned emotions of a significant move were bottled up and combined with the tension that had grown between my mother and me. The only difference is that the decision to move to Texas for one year was a mutual one.

My mother had been faced with the reality of raising a teenage boy as a single woman. I was too old for physical punishment, and whenever she would try, we would simply look at each other with piercing eyes so as to avoid it going any further. A good tongue lashing didn't work, either. I would simply leave the house and come back much later, allowing us to settle our emotions. There was no real calculated wisdom on my part in these moments, though I had way too much respect for my mother to retaliate. In short, my mother had her way of dealing with hardships and challenges, I had my way of dealing with them, and we both needed a short amount of time apart.

A reasonable self-description of myself at the time was that of a youthful, easily angered, snarky, isolated, and private person. Carrying the potential for so many unknown changes at once left a significant impact on my psyche. What would the environment be like? How would the relationship between my pops and I work out, since I did not really know him all that well? How would I adjust to a new school? How would I get along in a house occupied by five individuals? How would I adjust to the relocation—miles away from my comfort zone?

Everything in life is at risk of change. Everything around us *and* about us is constantly evolving. Change is constant, and at its center we might find progression, regression, or perhaps aggression. The fundamental aspect to consider is not avoidance of change, but management of it. We get to choose whether or not to accept and embrace it.

Even now, I cannot unequivocally say whether the move was a net positive or a net negative. What I can say is that, overall, I am grateful for the experience and what I learned during that year.

There is absolutely nothing wrong with enjoying one's own company. No matter where it is—riding in a car with no music, at home with no television playing, taking a nice walk alone—there is revelation in isolation. Cal Newport says it this way: "More generally, the lack of distraction in my life tones down that background hum of nervous mental energy that seems to increasingly pervade people's daily lives. I'm comfortable being bored, and this can be a surprisingly rewarding skill."[8]

When you're alone, your mind can be in free-form mode—to create, meditate, and orchestrate your own desires and plans. Quiet time is home to revelations for a purpose-driven existence and the process and path to complete your goals and achieve your dreams. It is where we can hear and understand our thoughts and ideas for today and tomorrow alike. There are so many benefits to spending time alone that I would be willing to bet there are a limited number of people, if any, who have made any significant impact on our society while inundated with noise.

Of course, on the other side of that coin, being a loner or spending sustained periods of time in isolation is detrimental. There is wisdom and maturity in seeking help whenever we find ourselves having absolutely no appetite for social encounters. Never get too lonely, for an extreme state of isolation benefits no one. Maintaining that balance is hard but critical.

Because I did not mind being alone at times, you could usually find me in my room—especially when my mother would have friends over. I had no interest in fraternizing. During those times when I was alone, tucked away in my room, I would strategize about how to earn a few coins. I would dream about doing fulfilling work to earn a living later in life, knowing that one day, I would be a grown-up with the responsibility of taking care of a family. The sound of nothing brought me a level of peace that surpassed even my understanding. When I moved to Texas, however, I did not have space for that degree of isolation. And boy, oh, boy did I miss my time alone.

I will note here that the word "noise" comes from the Latin word "nausea," which originally meant seasickness. The meaning then evolved to refer to any unwanted sound. The question then becomes, how can anyone reach that purposeful stage of creativity if there is a constant barrage of nauseating noise?

During my stay in Texas, my pops was wedded with three kids—two boys and one girl. All of us kids, now including me, were within one to four years apart in age. I will say that I was never thought of as their step-brother. From the outset, they received me as their brother. It was simply time for me to level up, in a vastly different environment than my cachet in middle school.

My siblings in Texas were extremely talented in sports, music, cooking, and comedy. They were also just as clever, mischievous, and rebellious as I was, or just as any other teenager for that matter. There was sibling rivalry, played out in sports and physical disagreements. There were drastic actions taken when one would get the best of the other. There were swift calculations of consequences when particularly vigorous tussling left damage in the house, figuring out quickly how to explain or rationalize away any further consequences.

But the environment was vastly different than that of my home in Louisiana. Here, there was neither room nor time for isolation. Someone was always at the house, and there was always some sort of action going. The stark realism of my move hit harder than it had during sporadic summer visits. A new state, a new school, a new church, a new routine, and the list goes on.

In early high school, my attention was on basketball. Those basketball handles and a decent mid-range jump shot won me a starting spot on the ninth- and tenth-grade A team, and I quickly became friends with a Caucasian kid who shared my love for the sport. I make the point of my friend being a Caucasian kid because up until then, I had never been friends with someone of any other race. We were from vastly different backgrounds, and I was getting a crash course in how to avoid stereotyping. I had to learn to assess people based on their actions and decisions rather than castigating an entire race of people. Because I did not know or understand the value of relationships regardless of skin color during these formidable years, I was skeptical of any other race that did not look like me. The misfortune for Black people is that, in many cases, the detrimental actions and decisions made by one Black person often casts a perception on our entire race. My skepticism could have easily metastasized into contempt had I not had this exposure. What I have learned is that it is hard to amass contempt for what you earnestly seek to try and understand, and this can only be cultivated through exposure.

Whenever I would visit his home, his family was very accepting. As I can remember, they were professors and teachers by trade. I recall the plethora of books inside the house, as well as the sound of peace that comes from not having to deal with financial deprivation. At least, that was the case as far as my eyes could see—their big, beautiful home, tucked away in a quaint community, with big healthy oak trees lining the streets was unlike any place I'd ever stayed. His parents definitely played a part in cultivating my developing thoughts about assessing individuals based on their actions and decisions alone.

His father had bought a basketball goal and placed it in the driveway towards the back of the house, so we would play one-on-one basketball well into the midnight hour. Sometimes, later than that. I played at the point guard position and he played the forward position, roughing each other up and honing our skills. A little heavier and taller than me, he had a fierce competitive streak that matched my own. Neither of us liked to lose, so we would go on into the night, refusing to relent in defeat. When we had the good fortune to play alongside each other on the school basketball team, the time we spent together was evident in our two-man game. Going up against other schools was easy in comparison.

We had practiced against each other so mercilessly that playing in the actual game was just plain ole fun. And it wasn't like the competition was stale—talk about leveling up. The sheer number of athletic basketball and football players coming out of Dickinson, Texas, was astonishing.

Aside from basketball, I found another home in the structure and order of the ROTC. In the short period I was part of this society, I quickly learned the power of uniformity and consistency. I learned about servant leadership and how following directions was just as important as leading and giving direction. I also confirmed my thinking and observations on how clothes should fit a man: neat, aligned, pressed, and with polished shoes, always.

I also noticed that this society did not carry the reverence or esteem it should have. With a lack of guidance or insight otherwise, during certain periods of the school day I would replace my ROTC uniform with my basketball uniform as quickly as possible. I guess I wanted to be known more for my athletic prowess of being a basketball player rather than for ROTC.

I had no real understanding or knowledge of the vast possibilities of a military career, which left me with no desire to be a part of the esteemed society of, for example, the US Military Academy (West Point) after high school. So, unfortunately, I did not last very long in ROTC, and basketball became my sole focus. It was go hard or go home, and I decided to go hard with basketball.

Take note of teachable moments.

Vital statistics suggest that the prominent Biblical characters of Ruth and Naomi's existence on earth fell sometime between 1375 and 1050 B.C. Ruth was Naomi's daughter-in-law, and their story begins after Naomi's husband and two sons die. This left the matriarch, Naomi, in a foreign land with only her daughter-in-law by her side.

Ruth had the opportunity to go back to her homeland after her husband's death, but she elected to stay by Naomi's side, stating, "Don't urge me to leave you or to turn back from you. Where you go, I will go, and where you stay, I will stay. Your people will be my people and your God my God. Where you die, I will die and there I will be buried. May the Lord deal with me, be it ever so severely, if even death separates you and Me" (Ruth 1:16-17).

To the extent that a daughter-in-law would be willing to reject her generational culture to stay with her mother-in-law speaks volumes about each woman's character. In our society, it is a common occurrence for a woman to be cynical or even demonstratively negative about her mother-in-law. But no, not Ruth. It was just the opposite. Naomi obviously made an impact on her family and community by the contents of her character. Similarly, Naomi—a matriarch who was full of life experiences—was principled enough to share, guide, nurture, and teach through love and a stern hand of correction.

As the matriarch of the family, my pop's wife made her own impression, with some shrewd but applicable life lessons. I affectionately referred to her as "Mums" using the British vernacular and spelling, reserving the term "Mama" in deference to my own biological mother. Like Naomi, Mums had a presence that filled any room she was in. She also had a very unorthodox way of teaching life lessons, though this made them absolutely memorable. Depending on the person, one could categorize these lessons as extreme or one could react to the lessons as good preparation for adulthood and the real world. I personally saw her style as the latter.

She had a way of being very intentional with instructions, just the same as Naomi did, providing Ruth with guidance and instructions for where to work and who to work with so she would not get hurt. Both of them, wise in counsel. Both entirely unselfish when it came to guiding and encouraging others. As such, the entire family looked to Mums for counsel.

After just a few months of Mums and I adjusting to my arrival to Texas, I never again heard her refer to me as her stepson or "my husband's son." No, I was her son, and I went on to respect her immensely for this. While Mums certainly had her flaws, just as we all do, here I will focus only on the lessons she taught me both directly and indirectly. These nuggets of wisdom were gifts that I am honored to now pass on to you.

One of the first lessons from Mums helped me understand the importance of appreciation for even the simpler things in life, as well as the impact of generosity. At fifteen years old, I was the youngest of the three boys. My brothers were sixteen and seventeen years old, respectively. They both had jobs already, and I had picked up a summer job at Pizza Hut. We all enjoyed working and making money, to the extent that our little minimum wage jobs gave us a boss-like complex. We had money in our pockets and could buy what we wanted. Our sister, on the other hand, did not have a job. She was home most of the time. Since Mums and my pops were working as well, Mums would often get our sister to help by cooking meals. Mums was a phenomenal cook and had taught our sister how to cook just the same, though she was only a few months behind me in age.

One particular afternoon, Mums asked each of us boys to give our sister some of our earnings since our sister was helping around the house and making our meals. However, in light of our skewed perceptions of being bosses and making money, we each made the decision to ignore this directive. We were not going to share any of our earnings with our sister. In our immaturity, we were convinced that, if our sister wanted money, she needed to go out and earn her own. We paid no attention to the value she was already providing by helping to keep cooked food in our bellies. And the doomsday response to these perceptions was soon to come.

Mums patiently waited for a day in which each of us boys were at work at the same time. When the time came, Mums removed all the toiletries that she had bought from our shared bathroom, including the toothpaste, toilet paper, soap, shampoo, deodorant—yes, *all of it*. She even removed all the bath towels. An eerie feeling filled the air by the time we got off work that night. Once home and ready for a good, hot shower, we saw the source of our unease. Mums looked at each of us without sympathy for our surprise and said, "Since you boys were not willing to generously share your earnings with your sister, you will need to buy your own food, buy your own soap, and buy your own towels."

This was a fast reality check on how life really works! I suppose we had felt like our money was our money and our parents' money was everyone's money. Aren't parents supposed to provide? In some ways, I reason this is true; however, there is something to be said for both generosity and non-monetary value. It only took a few days of going without showers and having to buy all our own toiletries to voluntarily reach into our pockets and give our sister as much or more than Mums had originally asked us to give. We also offered profuse apologies. This lesson was a powerful and profound one—a small price to pay for a huge dose of reality.

Whilst Mum's actions may be considered extreme to some, I appreciated the lesson. She taught me that it does not take much to be appreciative of and thankful for the people in our lives. Along these lines, Mums also ensured that we consistently gave to the church out of our earnings. She never really verified our giving—she simply stated (on many occasions) "make sure to give your tithes and offerings" when we went to church.

These lessons taught me the beauty in being a giver. Even now, I am a disciplined manager of money and consistently give to the church for the purpose of touching peoples' lives in a positive, encouraging, and uplifting way. I give consistently to both of my alma maters of Southern University in Baton Rouge and the University of St. Thomas in Houston, Texas. I give to help family members who have fallen on hard times.

I give to causes and events that are bigger than me, without expectations, and I have found that this generosity has been a gift to my own soul.

Some of the wealthiest people in the world are huge philanthropists. As phenomenal as it is, it has been reported that even Warren Buffet himself has publicly pledged to leave more than 99 percent of his estate to philanthropic causes. There is beauty in thinking about more than just our own self. Whether we recognize it this way or not, giving is a demonstration of appreciation, thankfulness, and love. Regardless of the amount, giving out of what you have is a sacrifice that does not go unnoticed.

The second lesson Mums taught me was about respecting parental authority and valuing time. Here are some details you need to know before this lesson will make sense: My brothers were both well known in the school circuit and in the neighborhood, and they had a reputation to protect. So, whenever there were major teenage gatherings and functions, they had to flex and be in the house—that is, wherever the function was. My oldest brother also had a small blue Volkswagen Beetle with a manual transmission that he had allowed me to start learning how to drive. That blue Volkswagen Beetle made it through some tough times—car crashes, fights, and all.

Now, one afternoon, we had asked Mums if we could go to a function, and the answer was no. Being as clever as we thought we were, we waited until around 12 a.m., after Mums and our pops went to bed and it was our time to go party. Then we each crawled out the window, quietly but clumsily, and pushed the Beetle out of the driveway without starting the engine. Once we thought we were a safe distance down the road, we started her up and took off down to Galveston, Texas, and our forbidden destination.

We had a great time, too. Sometime around 4 a.m., we made it back to Dickinson, turned the engine off, and pushed the Volkswagen Beetle back into the driveway, as close as possible to its previous resting place. We were sound asleep by 5 a.m.—and by 5:15 were awakened by a loud buzzing sound. It was an alarm clock that we had not set and would not have set under any circumstances, much less these. Mums had somehow known we had left the house and set the alarm accordingly. By 5:30 a.m., we had our clothes on and were trying to process her instructions that "this morning is yard day."

She had one-upped us, and we mowed the lawn and pulled the weeds accordingly. She didn't have to talk to us about the night before. The message was clear: If you can party all night, then you can work all day. I imagine she had counted the costs for us had something gone wrong in Galveston, and the answer was most likely the reason she originally said no to us going. She probably saw us pushing the car out of the driveway that night, yet she allowed us to carry on and assume the risk ourselves, knowing that there would be a teachable moment to come no matter how the night turned out. Perhaps this was extreme as well, but the lesson of "thou shalt obey your parents" became more real that day than it ever had before.

The long-term application of this lesson landed on leadership—how can anyone lead if they are unable to follow basic instructions, whether you agree with the instructions or not? Mums' leadership was often challenging but always done with care. In this case, for example, she showed me that good leaders allow for a reset after mistakes. We had made so many mistakes that night, and she led us through them and helped us manage them. Devoid of hurting yourself or someone else, the ability to follow instructions is critical.

Through this lesson, I came to understand the value of time and was slowly learning the concept of counting the costs of decisions. So much so, I now look at time as royalty. Time is the one commodity we can never get back. Hence, you are to value other people's time just the same as you value your time. Both are important. You see, I am a big proponent of working hard and playing hard, as well as taking time to rest. That fifteen minutes of sleep between returning home, falling asleep and being awakened to do chores was simply not enough. If we had followed directions, we could have spent that time doing some other youthful, fun activities instead of punishing chores. All in all, I learned a simple lesson: my time has to drive my actions versus my actions driving my time.

The final and most important to highlight from Mums was the value of relationships and the importance of salvation. Mums was a devoted Christian, and she demonstrated that by being in the Word of God and sharing it regularly. During my time in Texas, we were in church on Tuesdays for Bible study and again on Sunday mornings before church for Women's Group, Men's Group, or Youth Group, then church services afterwards. During summertime, we also attended a Christian summer camp for a month. Simply put, we were always in and around church. We attended church back in Louisiana, but never this much.

One day, Mums came to me and asked how I would feel about being baptized, which is a significant act in the Christian faith. I didn't know much in my fifteen-or-so years, but this much I knew: if it was good enough for Jesus to do, then it was certainly good enough for me to do as His "follower." Once again, if you are unable to follow, then how can you lead? As soon as Mums asked, I said yes without hesitation.

Mums personally reached out to my mother and asked if it was okay to have me baptized, and my mother also said yes without hesitation. She was all for anything that might improve my life—a mother's love on display. This moment also speaks to the beautiful relationship my mother and Mums had. Whenever they communicated, they were not cordial just to be cordial. They had a real reverence for each other. They valued their relationship out of love for me. And boy, am I grateful they did.

You cannot get very far in life without relationships or money. Relationships can open doors, so can money. Relationships can be used as a role to Bless others, so can money. In my view, there is no such thing as "self-made." We all need quality people in our orbit. Those who operate in wisdom know this to be a fact—we all need to cultivate relationships to reach a desired state.

Once again using the analogy of sports, you can always tell which teams have good internal relationships. They have chemistry. They move and share the ball unselfishly. They recognize that they need each other to win. During the 2015 NBA finals, the Golden State Warriors defeated the Cleveland Cavaliers for the championship. The following 2015-16 season, the Warriors posted the best ever regular season record of seventy-three wins and nine losses. The roster comprised the big three—Stephen Curry, a 6'2" point guard; Klay Thompson, a 6'5" shooting guard; and Draymond Green, a 6'6" power forward. All of them, for the most part, were undersized players comparatively speaking. But they were accompanied by significant role players, including but not limited to players such as Andre Iguodala, Harrison Barnes, Shaun Livingston, and others.

Over the years, Draymond would recognize the stellar shooting prowess of both Stephen and Klay, acknowledging Stephen Curry as the best basketball shooter of all time and

Klay as a consistent basketball marksman and two-way player. (Meaning, not only did Klay shoot well, but he was also a fierce defender.) Draymond was one of the primary ball distributors in the game at the time and had no problem sacrificing his stats, particularly offensively, for the team's sake. Draymond explained that "having a player like Stephen Curry, if I can get Stephen Curry the ball for a f*****g shot, why would I shoot?" This was someone recognizing he needed the help of someone else to be great.

As a teenager, I developed an unusual observation of the dynamics of relationships. I paid attention to actions and reactions. I paid attention to happiness and hurt, and I paid attention to how people used authority. Here's what I learned: Being in or developing a thankworthy relationship can be a force for good—for you and for the other person. Most of my relationships with my buddies, family members, and teachers were great, and I valued those connections. The relationship I cultivated with my tenth-grade basketball comrade, the relationship I had witnessed between my mother and Mums, the relationship between my mother and her patients (particularly Mr. Kantrow), the relationship between my mother and Elliot, the relationship between my pops and I—all of them were teaching me one thing: Relationships are a powerful, incalculable force.

Where you spend your money, I do believe, speaks to your values—and who you spend your time with does just the same. It takes work and wisdom to be prudent as to when to draw closer in a relationship and when to back away. An individual's relationship with money is also a forceful and powerful dynamic, and it takes work and wisdom to be prudent about earning it, investing it, saving it, and spending it.

Who we spend our time with reflects who we identify with and value. Just the same, where we spend our money and what we spend our money on demonstrates what we value. Relationships mirror the force of money—you can focus too much or not nearly enough on either. I had memorable encounters with people like Mr. Kantrow, who had enough money to be able to afford to have around-the-clock private nurses at his beautiful, modern, contemporary home, and I had memorable experiences of not having enough money and having to get public assistance. When we focus too much on money, we can easily slide into greed and corruption and idolizing it; when we're not focusing enough on it, we can unwittingly set ourselves up for a poverty-driven life. There must be a balance.

The same goes for relationships: when we focus too much on certain relationships, it becomes a distraction, leaving little to no time to focus on our own thoughts and ideas. Not focusing enough on certain relationships limits our potential for growth and the development of a healthy social compass.

As I reflect on my experiences and offer them as a different perspective for you to consider, know that each of these experiences with relationships and money and my own decisions were unknowingly gearing me up for turbulent times to come. I came to lean heavily on these experiences as I moved into young adulthood, and I needed them all for the massive transition ahead.

III

MISSTEPS AND TRANSFORMATION

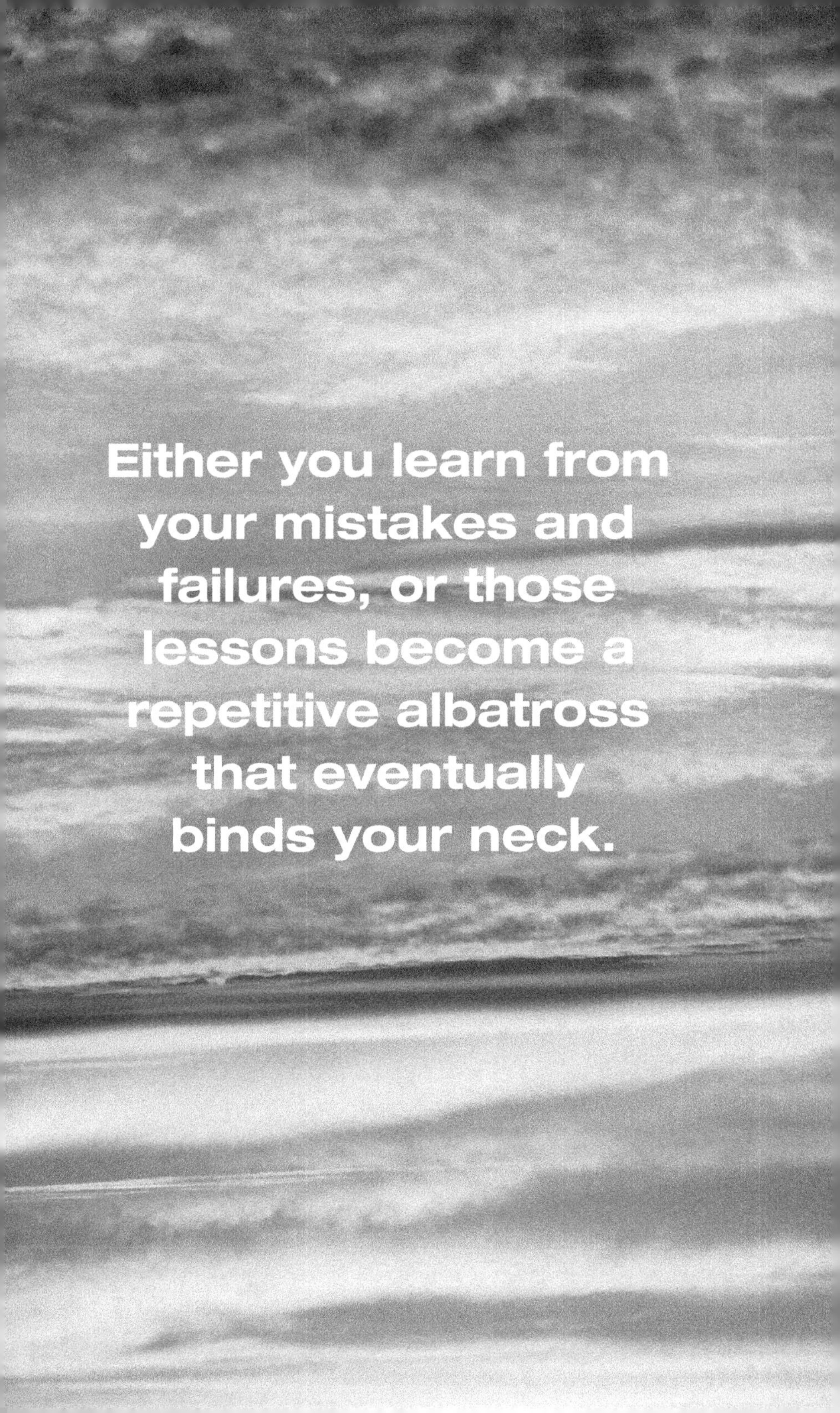

Either you learn from your mistakes and failures, or those lessons become a repetitive albatross that eventually binds your neck.

My decisions today impact my tomorrow.

The decisions we make drive our outcomes and become the basis of our existence. The decision to love, the decision to have children, the decision to serve God, the decision to go to school, the decision about a place of work, the decision to relocate, the decision to eat healthy and exercise, the decision around who to be friends with. We make hundreds of decisions a day, and over time, we begin to look and feel like those decisions.

Because our decisions elucidate the core of who we are, we must take time to evaluate the pros and cons, allowing for the brain and the heart to align before we move. We must also be mindful that not making a decision is, in fact, a decision. For example, if my car has a malfunction and there is not a car shop that can diagnose the problem, I have to decide whether or not to get another car. If I do not move on the decision to purchase another car, then I have inherently *decided* to live with the problem.

Sometimes, indirect decision-making will impact you—that is, decisions that are not directly yours but do impact you. Well, this is when we pray, we pivot, and we make peace. I think about our decisions in this way: when they turn out positive and constructive, it is because of grace (undeserved favor), and when they turn out poorly, we must consciously ask for grace. Through it all, I have come to the conclusion that it is prudent to seek God in our decisions, big and small, and as much as possible, learn to be content with the outcomes.

Good or bad, when God is in any of our individual decisions, the outcome rests with Him.

After one year in Texas, my mom and I decided that I would return to Louisiana. Throughout the long, boring, 4.5-hour drive, I experienced all sorts of emotions, with anxiety leading the way. It seemed that even the air smelled different in Louisiana. I was returning to my roots, with that big, loud, yellow apartment complex waiting for me. I was also brimming with excitement to hug my mother. I could not wait to hear what jokes or sharp, witty comments she had brewing. My appreciation for my mother had grown even more over that year. I was coming to the realization that she was Superwoman. She was doing it all as a single mother to two kids—working, cooking, providing, sheltering, and all with no complaints of life's hardships. The woman was simply great at being a steward of her responsibility. When I left, it seemed she had needed a break. But on my return, her world was revived.

As soon as my feet hit the ground in Louisiana, my primary focus was to reconnect with friends, especially the girls and my homeboys. The second order of business was to compete for a starting spot at the point guard position for the varsity basketball team. Before the season started, there had been a splash in the local newspaper indicating that a 6'0" guard had returned to Louisiana—me, though my height had been embellished by a couple of inches, as often happens for athletes—cementing my spot as the starting point guard at Istrouma High School.

Before the start of the season, practices were long, physical, and competitive. In some cases, we were doing two-a-day practices—early in the morning before school started and late in the afternoon at the end of the school day. Practices were intentionally driven to make you quit. If you did not love basketball, this was not the place for you. However, given that this school was in a rough part of town, it was rare that anyone actually would quit. You either made the team or you were cut. Otherwise, quitting was simply not an option. Being labeled a quitter in school would make you the butt of many jokes and non-stop taunting. Even more than the threat of social pressure, I had such an aura of stubbornness that quitting never ever crossed my mind. If I started a sport or a project, there was no turning back. I was going to finish. This also meant I had better do my homework upfront about whatever I was going to engage in. Once I was in it, I was in it.

The decision to migrate back to Louisiana, albeit far removed from the fame and notoriety of "The Decision" by Lebron James to move from Cleveland to Miami, still felt significant. I could only imagine the pressure this young man faced. How many of us can remember July, 2010, when Lebron James made the decision to leave the Cleveland Cavaliers and join the Miami Heat? The ESPN sports network aired a televised special, and at the tender age of roughly 25 years old, Lebron James spoke to an audience of tens of millions, telling them that he was "taking his talents to South Beach" to join the Miami Heat. Some considered the decision to be unwise and selfish.

As one of the greatest talents the game has ever seen, there were suggestions that this decision shifted the balance of the talent in the whole National Basketball Association. The Cleveland Cavaliers team owner at the time, Dan Gilbert, publicly called Lebron's decision "a shameful display of selfishness and betrayal." The fallout from the fans in Cleveland was tremendous, including burning Lebron jerseys on national television. Meanwhile, there are also reports of decisions that were made behind the public decision. Some reports suggested that Lebron had repeatedly tried to work with the new Cavaliers management to recruit new and good players to win championship titles. After Lebron's efforts failed, and considering the growing status of free agency that allowed players to have more control over their own destiny, he decided the best decision for himself would be to move cities.

Who knows if his decision—or any decision—was ultimately good or bad. Once again, when our decisions turn out positive and constructive, it is because of grace, and when our decisions turn out poorly, we must consciously ask for grace.

Istrouma High School was an all-Black high school in one of the toughest parts of the city of Baton Rouge. Our rivalries with other tough schools, such as Capitol High School and McKinley High School in Baton Rouge, brought fierce physical competition. Our guys were big, long, physical, fast athletes, and we all played free of drugs—at least as far as I knew. This was an accomplishment of our father-like, strict, combative, foul-mouthed head coach. If you messed up, the correction came immediately, typically with harsh expletives.

We played *fast*. Coming off the rebound from the center or forward, the "bigs" would pass the ball to the wing of a crossing point guard to ignite the fast break. Then the point guard had one of three options: take it all the way to the hoop, pass to a teammate on either the left or right lanes for an easy layup, or reset for a designed play in the front court. If you did not run with the point guard to finish the fast break, all hell would break loose from the sidelines. Play would immediately stop, the non-hustling player would get a tongue lashing, and then we would all have to "run suicide drills." This was a drill that required you to start running at the baseline, run to the free throw line, then run back to the baseline. After that, you'd run to half court and back. After that, run to the opposite free throw line and back. After that, run the full court, down and back. This would go on until the coach said we could stop, and it would repeat until we were mistake free. Ultimately, the conditioning from this drill made sure we could just about do a defensive full court press for most of (if not all of) a game. We always kept up the pressure. If you got tired, you were subbed out immediately. It was fun but intensive.

One of our archrivals, McKinley High School, were also big, long, physical, and fast. They played loose and free, conceivably because most if not all of them were playing "high"—you could smell the weed a mile away. One night, I had the challenge of guarding this one guy for most of the game, where I would flare out to the wing on the left side to contest the shot, and he pulled up to take it, and all I could smell was weed.

Some nights, some guys are just in a zone for shooting, and so it was for him in that game. He scored twenty-plus points, with little that I or anyone else from our team could do to stop him. Just before half-time, one of our star players (who was having an off night for shooting) turned the ball over at a critical time in the second quarter. During halftime, the coach was so enraged that he reached out and slapped that star player—and it changed the dynamics of our play in the third and fourth quarter. Corporal punishment was not unusual in the 1980s. I'm not sure if it was *legal*, but it was certainly not unusual. Some parents were okay with it if it was a corrective action taken to change a kid's behavior. In any case, we put up a competitive fight for the rest of the game, then ultimately lost it anyway.

I will say that the environment of sports and education has changed so dramatically in this day and age that kids now feel perfectly okay to inflict "corporal punishment" on teachers and administrators. Could this be one of the reasons there is a growing shortage of teachers and administrators in today's society? Could it come from the lack of spiritual reminders in the school system? Could it be from a lack of funding in certain areas of a city? Maybe it is a combination of multiple factors.

Few of the athletes on our team, including myself, had parents in the stands. My mother had no interest in sports and perhaps did not know how important basketball was to me, and my pops lived in another state. Hence, my parental fan base was null and void throughout both junior high school and high school. Still, I excelled at the sport at the high-school level, leaving no room for excuses or feeling sorry for myself. Later in life, when I had my own children, I recognized the impact of a lack of fan base from my family as a youngster. I became the coach for all their athletic engagements or participated as their Uber driver—albeit "Uber" was not around during this time. It was undeniable that I would be present.

*Education is a worthy endeavor at
every stage in life; never stop learning.*

Every child deserves the right of a quality education, especially during their most impressionable years. Yet, as a result of inadequate and inconsistent funding for public education, the average level of education in America is a high school diploma, with only 34 percent of the American population boasting a four-year college degree. Level funding for education, regardless of zip codes, says to all our children that they are precious American citizens for whom we set high expectations.

Why is education so important? Among other things, at its base, education infuses confidence, assists in providing a way to make a living, sparks curiosity to better understand the world in which we live, leaves a rich legacy of achievement, teaches an aspect of discipline and perseverance, and opens the doors to opportunity. In more ways than one, it literally pays to invest in education, as it ultimately lifts and expands our economy.

Several years after I left my high school, it closed for a period of time—seemingly due to lack of funding, a shortage of willing and qualified teachers and administrators, and ongoing violence. As one of the world's biggest economic engines, the only way to maintain innovation is to educate our population, regardless of where they live.

Our moral compass can be absolutely influenced and corrupted by corrupt people. That is, we are to be mindful of the company we keep.

Our small apartment could not have been more than 1,000 square feet, each room boasting no more than 100 square feet except for the master bedroom, which I think was just a little bigger. The kitchen was just to the right as you walked through the front door, with barely enough room to get more than two people in the kitchen at one time. Just beyond it was the living area, with sliding back doors that led into a small open area facing the back of the next set of apartments. From the front door and about ten feet in, turning left would lead to the bedrooms. Everything was just as I remembered it when I left for Texas, only now there were side-by-side twin beds in my old room. My cousin had asked my mom if he could move in, given his tumultuous relationship with his own mother.

The dynamics between my cousin and his mother were not healthy. Interestingly, I noticed over many years that my mother loved his mother from a distance. She never got too close to his mother, only close enough to be there if she was needed in some way. So, not one to turn away family, my mother allowed my cousin to move in, thinking that giving him a new environment and a fresh start would be good for him.

My cousin was just about the same size as me, if just a bit heavier. It was not a problem for either of us to get around the two beds in our now-shared room. Plus, he never really went to school consistently. He loathed school and everything about it. He was also a natural fighter with the heart of a lion—trouble seemed to find him no matter where he was. At the time, this combination made him a subtle menace to society. Over time, he became a grave menace to society.

In the late 1980s, the music industry had produced some steamy and, in my view, well-written love ballads, and the hip-hop genre was becoming ever more popular. In other words, listening to music was a great pastime. One of our all-time favorite music groups was New Edition. Every kid who thought they could sing wanted to be like New Edition. Any work I could do, I would spend a significant portion of the money I earned on audio cassette tapes. They were developed by the Dutch company Phillips, and you could purchase these tapes with pre-recorded music content. For recording my own music (mixed tapes), my brand of choice was the Maxell Compact Cassette, and I had amassed a *ton* of them.

I kept a plethora of these tapes in a few shoe boxes underneath my bed, and my cousin and I would listen to them well into the evening. On occasion, we would invite acquaintances—not necessarily friends—to hang out and listen to music. Lo and behold, one day we came home to the apartment to see that half the tapes were gone. Someone had stolen some of my favorite music, and my anger was through the *roof.* My cousin was right there, too, fanning the flames and stirring the pot, encouraging my hostility. "You cannot just let this go." "Whoever stole the tapes broke the code." "We gotta make a statement and make them pay." He kept going on and on, my anger ever increasing. Then he said the magic words:

"We will find the person who stole the tapes, and together we will *destroy* them."

We looked high and low for the cassette tapes. We probed and posed questions to everyone we had allowed to listen to them. Soon, we found the young man who had stolen the cassette tapes. He lived just three apartment doors down the hallway and had somehow gotten himself into our apartment, where he knew exactly where to find the cassette tapes. When we knew for sure it was him, we invited him to hang out. Our plan was for him and I to brawl it out whilst my cousin ensured no one else could jump in. We executed that plan, and then my cousin finished him with a few kicks to the abdomen. By the time it was all done, the young man had to be taken to Earl K. Long Hospital for his injuries, that same charity hospital I'd been familiar with as a kid, just down the street.

Up to that point, I had effectively avoided courts and crime. Until that young man pressed charges for criminal assault. My unchecked anger and enhanced ego ultimately landed me in front of a judge. Since it was my first time being entangled in the criminal justice system, the judge handed me probation and community service. Since my cousin and his mom had experience maneuvering through the justice system in these types of situations, he successfully navigated his way through the process without any consequences for his part.

From there forward, my relationship with my cousin became as distant as the West Coast is from the East. I knew that my association with him would eventually land me in even hotter water with the justice system, and I no longer wanted anything more to do with him. Not long after, my mother asked my cousin to move back with his mother, unwilling to risk her son getting into more trouble. Once again, my mother loved her sister from a distance. They just saw the world differently.

Although no one can make us do anything, the lesson I learned here was that one small lapse in judgment can make way for us to fall for anything. My lapse in judgment with regards to the cassette tapes could have cost me months or years in jail, after years of staying clear of serious trouble. We must count the cost and the impact as much as we can before making life-altering decisions.

*Trouble is very easy to get into but can
be extremely difficult to get out of.*

The 1994 Crime Bill passed on the notion that violent crime had reached an all-time high. Whilst the bill had several reasonable-sounding provisions in it, like reducing the number of firearms on the streets and increasing the number of law enforcement officers, it is now and was then public knowledge that the bill had a pernicious effect as well. It allocated billions in funding to states across the country, for them to increase the number of prison beds for those committing violent crimes.

There are many politicians on record indicating that they knew the bill significantly contributed to our already massive incarceration rate. Bill Clinton stood before congress in January 1994 saying that "we need to be tough and smart on crime." Senator Joe Biden suggested that the bill was a very significant one, and he was right. The bill's new sentencing laws were seen as the answer to repeat offenders who were considered a menace to society. Bill Clinton said that if you committed a third crime you would "be put away, and put away for good; three strikes and you are out." In most states, all three strikes had to be violent or serious crimes; in other states, any kind of crime, even the lowliest among them, made you eligible for the "three strikes law." This put several hundreds of thousands of low-level offenders in prison for life.

Several years after the law was enacted, data suggests that a sizable percentage of the "three strikes" inmates were serving

25-to-life sentences for non-violent crimes, many of whom were individuals who had been caught up in the epidemic of drug abuse. There was also an astounding impact on the mentally ill and homeless. For all intents and purposes, the law's unintended consequences led to today's estimates of more than two million individuals incarcerated in the United States. The United States now has the world's largest prison population, at a staggering cost of more than $80 billion dollars a year.[9]

The crime bill hit close to home. During this time period and a few years thereafter, my cousin's crimes increased in number and viciousness. I watched from afar, taking mental notes and trying hard to keep my explosive anger and ego in check. I personally started moving differently, conscientious about the company I was keeping, being as judicious as possible when on the night scene, and staying busy with school and basketball. I had very much developed a sixth sense for watching other peoples' circumstances and situations escalate and could quickly assess, apply, and pivot when needed. Today, that very same cousin who I had shared meals and a home with is now serving 99 years to life in prison, ensnared by the three strikes law.

My thoughts on the 1994 crime bill: the problem of crime both then and now is a very nuanced issue. Legislating crime is much like the doctor prescribing medicine. That is to say, the medicine prescribed by the doctors very well may solve your infirmity while at the same time carrying unintended side effects. I understand the thought behind the "three strikes" for violent crime; however, when the lowliest crimes started getting lumped in with it, the scope creep of change without proper control, adding new laws or provisions outside of the original law, led to unintended consequences.

The side effect of the 1994 crime bill proved to be costly mass incarceration, ultimately evolving to the many private prisons that are now operating for profit. Further, I deeply hurt for those who suffer from mental illness and are homeless. Unfortunately, the people who fall into this segment of the population are often impacted by laws such as these. In many cases, rather than getting assistance for mental illness, they are instead sent into the penal system.

Once again, crime and how to solve for it is a very nuanced issue. It truly requires thoughtful and pragmatic leadership, including politicians who can legislate with the heart *and* the head. Lofty rhetoric from both the Democratic and Republican parties simply does not do the American citizenry any good.

Every single human being walking the face of this earth will make mistakes, and we are all one decision away from changing our family's lives for the good for many generations or wrecking our lives and ripping our families apart for many generations. This is why it is so important to give and receive grace.

I got the call in February 1989.

"Carnell, I'm pregnant. We are having a baby."

That rotary-dialed phone went quiet for several seconds.

I can only describe my emotions in that moment as happy, bewildered, and dismayed all at the same time. This continued for the months that sped by afterward, until all I could feel was numb. Life was moving fast, and I was in a daze. I truly needed a male figure in my life with wisdom and integrity. Someone to call for guidance and advice. My mother was supportive; however, there was only so much she could do or say—the rest required strong male involvement. I had no such figure to turn to.

In November 1989, when I was just eighteen years old, my beautiful daughter was born. And I started to make the transition from boy to man. I had to navigate this uncharted territory by trial and error. It is where I learned two key words: responsibility and accountability. Not one to run from anything, I simply leaned in.

My daughter's mother and I were rapidly seeing the world very differently, keeping marriage off the table. So, while working and going to school, most of the money I earned was directed towards making sure my daughter was provided for. When my daughter was not with her mother, she was right there with me, wherever I would go. My hand of cover and protection was on her from the minute she was born. Ever mindful of who was around her to prevent any harm or abuse of any kind, I was very much overly protective of her as she grew. My mother was just the same with her, both protective and spending any discretionary money she had on her granddaughter.

The transition from boy to man was flat out hard. I had been working at a rehabilitation hospital in Baton Rouge, initially in the kitchen "busting suds," as the southern vernacular goes. Meaning, washing dishes. I also brought a younger cousin in with me, who could not have been more than thirteen years old at the time. It was my way of reaching back to pull a young male forward, with the intention of helping him make better decisions than I had in previous years. Incidentally, he is the younger brother to my cousin I had gotten into trouble with regarding those cassette tapes. As young as I was, he referred to me as a father figure—someone who was taking the time to teach him responsibility and accountability. In my own rudimentary and sophomoric way, I was trying to give him what I was longing for: the model of a man who holds wisdom and integrity.

The transition from boy to man was also rapid. I moved from the hospital kitchen to caring for patients on the hospital floor. I was pushing myself to want more out of life and to do more with my life, so I kept an eye open for any opportunity for upward progression from the hospital kitchen. Watching my mother care for patients had now become my work of choice. Soon, I became friends with an older lady who was responsible for scheduling and had significant influence with the nurses in charge and the hospital leadership. She ultimately became my sponsor, explaining the nuances of working in a hospital setting, helping me navigate the vicious comments some patients had, and securing for me as many hours of work that I could handle despite the political landscape of the hospital.

For patients young and old, Black and White, good bedside manners were the goal. However, some of the patients would make vile and derogatory comments to me and other Black people in charge of helping them get better. They'd make comments such as "I don't want any Blacks in my room," or "The Black people are trying to kill me with the medicines they are giving me." The list goes on and on. Nonetheless, the ends justified the means. I had a child to care for and bills to pay, so I had to keep my composure. On the other hand, my sponsor was skilled at addressing and handling such behavior and abuse without being as malicious as they were. She was firm in stating that such behavior would not be tolerated and that if the behavior continued, she would make it clear that she would do everything in her power to work with the hospital leadership to discharge the person and have them moved to another hospital.

My experience was not all bad. In addition to my sponsor, I also met a very kind and pleasant older man of Caucasian descent while working at the hospital. Moderately tall, soft-spoken, clean-cut—a statesman-like figure who was the Director of Procurement for the hospital. I was in the market for a car, and he happened to be selling his. It was a white, 1985, four-door Mercury Marquis. The interior was navy blue with cloth seats, and this car was clean. We went around and around on negotiating the price of the car for weeks, in what became my first official taste of negotiating. Some four months later, we landed on the price. I had managed to save just enough cash to purchase the car, and I negotiated the price so that I had some left over for other bills. Then I handed over the agreed-upon amount, we went through the administrative process to get titles changed over, and I was off with my new used car.

I thought I was too cool even for the winter.

The car was good on gas, so I was all over Baton Rouge in it. A few times, I even drove it to Houston and back. Oddly, I preferred driving at night, when traffic was free flowing with limited cars on the road. I would pop my cassette tapes in and it would just be me and my music, wherever I was going. Because I had spent my own money, I had an innate desire to keep it clean, the tires rotated, and the oil changed on a regular basis. But I had gone at it all alone, with no experience and no help with the negotiations, administration, or maintenance. I could not fail to mention that my sponsor at the rehabilitation hospital had initially introduced me to the gentleman who sold me the car. Even so, without further help with the car itself, I had to be self-taught. In other words, I asked a lot of questions.

It is a worthwhile endeavor to seek out a sponsor whom you trust in your world of work. Having a sponsor in the room to speak on your behalf is more than money can buy and can bring tremendous value to your progression. They should be seasoned with experience, a strong network, and influence with decision makers. Often, as the sponsor rises in seniority, they will bring along those they know and can vouch for. If you are not in the room as human resources are being discussed, you could certainly be on the agenda.

Having a mentor is also important. Look for someone who is extremely adept at and considered a subject matter expert at their job. They should know their job and organization well and be able to guide you on how to be successful at your job. Unlike a sponsor, they may not be in the room when human resources are being discussed, but they can educate you how to stay off the agenda as firing decisions are being made.

As the older lady at the rehabilitation hospital progressed, so did I. When pay raises happened, I would always receive at or above the payout range. Make no mistake—I was good at my job and earned every single nickel. I worked overtime whenever she had a shortage and needed someone to step in. I took on jobs that were not always in my scope. Nothing at the job was given to me. She was the absolute best at her job as well and happened to be an influential person at the hospital. Hence, when I did well at my job and made hers easier, I gained the luxury of a sponsor and a mentor all in one. This, in most cases, is rare.

The secret to self-awareness is to recognize what you don't know. No matter your age or lot in life, seek guidance or advice from someone with wisdom. Whether you're navigating the zigzagging road of parenthood, buying your first car, or maneuvering the nuances of the work world, seek the counsel of those you trust.

Eventually, my mother secured some savings and a high enough credit score to qualify to buy a small, 1,200 square-foot, three-bedroom house. Of course, my mother being my mother, she always made extra payments to the thirty-year principal when she could. I will never forget her pure happiness and exhilaration when the bank said they would approve the loan.

The location was somewhat of an upgrade from public housing, but not by a lot. It didn't take long for my mother to become the matriarch on the street where the house was located. People would stop in and simply say, "Ms. Gail, I saw your car outside, and I just wanted to check on you and see how ya doing." She loved having people around and would invite several folks over every time she came home with that good ole delicacy of hot boiled crawfish and shrimp, with sausage and corn included. I remember everyone sitting around the table with perspiration trickling from their noses, fingers greased with spices, and foreheads glistening with a slow, sticky sweat—all signs that the crawfish was done right.

For the many years my mother was there, I cannot remember a single time that her home was broken into or vandalized. Everyone watched her house when she was not there, and she returned the favor when they were gone. Many in the neighborhood also knew she was a no-nonsense woman, with her Magnum 357 nickel-plated pistol ever present, which was her preferred form of protection. Anytime there was some commotion or disturbance in the neighborhood, she would tell anyone sitting next to her, "Reach me my purse." This meant she needed to be close to what was inside the purse—that pistol—and we all knew it.

By now, Elliot was back in the picture (remember him?) and would stop in from time to time to say hello to my mother and check on my sister, his daughter. In fact, Elliot had a few reasons to make stops in the neighborhood. His best friend at the time happened to live two houses down, and they both worked as operators at one of the local chemical plants. Fortunately, my mother had found her stride and was now at peace. I saw the pride in my mother when she achieved home ownership—she smiled more, she worked even harder, and she kept a rolling invitation to anyone who wanted to visit her home. My mother did not carry an ego; however, she was very much a prideful woman, with enough humility to give her space to take pride in her accomplishments. I do not recall my mother basking in ego, or being overly arrogant or conceited. She had worked hard to accomplish a seemingly impossible feat. And remember, she was doing it all by herself. Home ownership had boosted her confidence and self-esteem.

Everyone has good and
bad character traits.

On a cool winter's day, after I had left for work, I got word that there had been an altercation between my sister and her boyfriend. Now, my mother, my sister, and I were a close-knit family and very much protective of each other when it came to external matters. Internally, our relationship was up and down. My sister was dating a guy a few years older than her. Later, I learned that he was also an unsavory character and was known in some circles as a troublemaker with violent tendencies. At the time, however, my antennas were simply up. I felt like I had something of an unrefined, animalistic, wolf-like behavior. That is, I wanted to protect my pack—my mother and my sister—by any means necessary. Sometimes, without thinking things through.

Some interesting facts about wolves: They would sacrifice their lives for family. Much like humans, wolves use body language—including eye contact, facial expressions, and body posturing—when there is a threat to them or the pack. They can analyze situations and adapt their strategies on the fly, demonstrating a high level of intelligence. Their deep loyalty to the pack ensures the entire family works together seamlessly, supporting injured and elderly wolves rather than abandoning them. The pack's cohesion allows them to take on challenges that they could not handle individually. This bond makes them a unified and powerful force.

My mother and I tried piecing the details together to understand what happened between my sister and her boyfriend.
As the story unfolded, the most disturbing part was that the
altercation had turned physical. My mother and I discussed
how we would address the issue, then decided to approach it
in two ways. First, we would call Elliot over to talk it through
since it involved his daughter. Second, we would invite the
young man and his mother over to look for common ground
and move forward without having to address a physical altercation ever again.

The young man and his mother made it over to my mother's home at roughly 6 p.m. that evening. My sister explained
her side, and her boyfriend explained his. Then, what started
out as a cordial conversation quickly took a turn for the worse.

Their voices elevated as both relayed their own views of
what happened. My mother stepped in and tried to reduce the
friction and find common ground between the two of them.
Unfortunately, the young man was not interested in a pragmatic or a sound resolution. It was as though he was unnec-
essarily looking for a reason to escalate the situation. His rage
quickly turned to visceral anger, even as my mother encouraged us all to calm down so that we could hear each other out.

At this point, the young man became even more disrespect-
ful. *His* mother did not budge or say a word through any of it,
almost as if she supported what he had just said. *My* mother
was always armed with her 357 nickel-plated pistol in her purse.
When I'd heard the disrespect espoused towards my mother, I
did not take kindly to it. That's when Elliot sprang into action
to de-escalate what was quickly becoming a pugnacious

situation. Needless to say, my actions that evening could have gotten me entangled with the judicial system for many, many years to come.

My ego had fanned the flames of my anger, and I allowed someone to instigate actions from me before I could fully think things through. I allowed someone else to have more control of my mentality than I did, and as a result, I made a violent and costly error in judgment. Had I taken "a pause and pivot" that day, it would have allowed me to have more mental control. I could have used sensible communication tactics, closed the meeting, and asked everyone to depart until emotions could settle down.

Given the young man's background, I knew he would come back with a vengeance; and that he did. Not long after, he came back with about six other guys with guns and other weapons. The police disbursed the congregating people and administered crowd control. Eventually, the street was quiet, and my sister's relationship with that young man was over.

Elliot, the man who was inconsistent at keeping his word, had saved me from catastrophic actions. Over the years, I had never disrespected Elliot, but I always kept him at arm's length. Elliot was adept and knew the "streets" very well, maneuvering them for years without making any headlines. The very man who I saw make promises and never keep them was ultimately willing to step in to prevent what could have turned out to be an awful incident. That night, I learned that everyone has elements of good and bad character traits. Allowing people to be who they are gives you the opportunity to determine how to engage with them (or not).

Years before, it would have never occurred to me that Elliot would become a saving grace for me. From then on, I chose to be cordial, setting aside my personal feelings for the sake of my mother and my sister. You simply never know who you may need, so it is wise to maintain composure and withhold judgment—particularly judgment that slams the content of a person's character. After all, we all have some innate character flaw. No one is perfect.

This incident taught me so many solemn lessons. One of which was a basic aversion to fighting or violence as a first reaction. In order for me to live and not die, I had to learn that my strength was in my ability to gauge a situation and decide how to proceed after fully counting the costs of my actions. I learned to practice patience and to think any situation through. I also had to learn that the statesman-like behavior that allowed a person to be effective and affective in any situation would not be embodied in my bravado, but rather in my ability to meet at the place of harmony and cooperation. I cannot say that I have fully perfected this skill, however, I work at it every day.

Learning from our decisions, both good and bad, is a part of the fabric of our being. When tragedy strikes, when the frailty of our human existence is paired with being the orchestrators of our own confusion, there is comfort in knowing there is a saving grace to be found in and around any decision. That saving grace operates in love, even when dark days befall us. It cultivates and makes space for our ingression to eternity.

In Hebrew, the root word for transformation is "hapak," which means to change, to turn about, or overturn. For me, that change came with a simple conversation with my friends, who were all discussing their plans for enrolling at Southern University and A&M College in Baton Rouge. The conversation caught my attention differently. Usually, our conversations were about sports, relationships, where we were going to hang out over the weekend, etc. Never anything about pursuing higher education. With no formal plans, I initially said I would roll with them over to Southern University when they went there to finish their administrative business. I remember thinking I was bored anyway and this gave me something to do.

My initial experience of being on the "yard"—that is, the Southern University campus—was new, fresh, and exhilarating. Seeing a plethora of folks who looked like me all pursuing higher education opened up a whole new frame of mind. The marching band and the football games in particular felt like the third coming in my world of experiences, if there could be one. What had started as a way to kill time for a day turned into a *very* long day, as I decided to enroll as well. I had not been sure of my next steps in life, and I knew it was time for a change. Being on that campus was like a light bulb going off. I could see that pursuing my education at the collegiate level would facilitate a much-needed transformation. To get where

I wanted to go, I was going to have to change my entire way of thinking, as well as my environment.

One thing I did *not* enjoy about that day on campus was the hour-plus wait in multiple lines to register for classes. This was, of course, before the age of information improved technology and automation. At the beginning of each semester, everyone would crowd into the F.G. Clark Activity Center ("the campus mini-dome") to get their classes assigned—a process that literally took all day.

I was a natural at managing money, so I decided to pursue business economics. On several occasions, folks had falsely accused me of selling drugs due to the financial status I appeared to have. That had never been the case. In fact, since I could not afford the cost of university, I had to apply for and receive Pell Grants. Those funds, plus my employment earnings from working at the rehabilitation hospital, helped finance my undergraduate tuition and books. I am grateful to our governmental system at the time that thought enough of me and other low-income students to provide where we had fallen short financially. I am especially grateful to Southern University, a Historically Black University (HBCU), for providing the opportunity for students of all colors and nationalities to study, and especially for those who look like me.

Southern University was one of the major driving factors in changing the course of my life. The camaraderie on campus, the independence and freedom to move about, the excitement of seeing everyone striving for the same goal of getting a degree. I went from absolutely loathing school to appreciating the many benefits of higher education. I like to say I "studied money" while I was there. The theory and application of how money works—supply and demand, monetary and fiscal policy—became my drug of choice, stirring up my appetite for *more*.

A few years into my studies, I applied for an internship with the Central Intelligence Agency (CIA) and the National Aeronautics and Space Administration (NASA). The latter prevailed, and I landed my first professional internship at the John C. Stennis Space Center, NASA's rocket testing facility housed in Mississippi. Because there were not many apartment complexes in the area, NASA had agreements with local homeowners to provide housing for interns. My host was a beautiful 70-plus-year-old woman who had a modest, clean, three-bedroom home. She welcomed me and another student, a young woman who was attending Mississippi State University and who quickly became my friend. We carpooled to NASA on most days and took turns cooking, though I could not cook and took us out to eat on most of my days.

Working at NASA was an absolutely cherished experience. The work was not hard—I was assigned to do general ledger reconciliations in the accounting department—just different from any other working experience I had up to that point. There, I began to learn the intricacies of working in corporate America. At the same time, once the workday was over, life was extremely boring. As you can probably imagine, the transition from moving about freely under the city lights of Baton Rouge, Louisiana, to being stationary in the rural backdrop of Picayune, Mississippi, was not easy. You could hear a nickel drop a mile away, it was so quiet. Notwithstanding, the educational and eye-opening experience working at NASA far outweighed the non-social existence of living in Picayune.

One day, on my way to my office building on the NASA campus, I passed two older ladies who worked in the same building. One of them said to me, "Where are you going in such a hurry?"

I replied almost over my shoulder, "I need to get to my office—I have got work to do."

She looked at me with a motherly smile, then said, "Keep living."

For years, I did not know what she meant. Eventually, I understood that there comes a day when you don't move as fast. She was inviting me to take my time and be present in the moment, because that will be more gratifying than the work. Eventually I wouldn't live to work, but rather work to live.

Our decisions, good and bad,
eventually come full circle.

My work in the accounting department at NASA was totally different than the accounting practices that were being taught at university. I had to learn and unlearn on both levels in order to keep my internship and successfully pass my classes. But by May of 1995, I had received my undergraduate degree in Business Economics.

One month before I graduated, the namesake for the campus where I interned—John Cornelius Stennis—passed away. He had been an American politician from the state of Mississippi, having served as a Democratic US Senator for over forty years. Most notably, John Cornelious Stennis had initially been for racial segregation. He voted against the Civil Rights Act of 1964, the Voting Rights Act of 1965, and the Civil Rights Act of 1968.[10] Now here I was, some thirty years after those "no" votes, working at a facility named after this gentleman who had been a staunch supporter of segregation.

Before graduating, I interviewed for several jobs on the Southern University campus and had gotten two other offers—one to return to John C. Stennis in Mississippi to work in procurement, and one from Shell Oil Company in Houston, Texas. My mindset throughout this decision was that I needed to secure gainful employment, with the ability to earn a substantial income so that I could be a solid provider for my daughter. After evaluating the quality of living in Texas versus Mississippi, the quality of education in Texas versus Mississippi, and the equality of pay in Texas versus Mississippi, I chose to march towards Houston, Texas. When the offer letter came in with a starting salary in the high upper twenties, my decision was finalized without hesitation.

Shell Oil Company had been on Southern University's campus because they were intentionally looking for minority talent. In that regard, I was one of many beneficiaries of the construct of Diversity and Inclusion initiatives. While not a perfect company, Shell truly believed in diversity and benefited from having a variety of voices at the corporate level, as reflected in its consistent ranking in the top quartile of energy companies. I went on to spend almost three decades there, including travel to seven different countries across South America, Europe, and the Far East, all on behalf of Shell Oil Company.

The earliest months, however, were spent getting my affairs in order, getting situated in Houston, and relocating my daughter to join me. Her mother and I agreed that there would be better opportunities for her in Texas versus Louisiana. Another full circle moment was complete, bringing me back to Texas just eight years after I'd left, this time as a father and not just as a son.

Had I lacked any previous exposure to Texas, it is plausible that I would have simply remained in Louisiana, a state I loathed for its lack of progress, poor diversity of industries, and corrupt political structure. My perception, and perhaps an aspect of reality, was that the gap between the rich and the working poor was as wide as the Atlantic Ocean. But because I had previous exposure to the city and state, as well as a support system in my pops and a couple of his brothers, a sister, and several cousins, moving to Houston had been the obvious choice. There were always massive family gatherings, cookouts, and plain ole fellowship. My pops had mastered the skill of barbecuing and frying turkeys, and there were very few cookouts without his own concoction of barbecue sauce on the menu.

Texas was opposite to Louisiana in almost every way. As one of the largest states in the US based on land mass, it had a plethora of housing and continues to grow much faster than the average state. It is also a conservative state, but my work and residence was conducted in Harris County, where voters are more ideologically diverse and closer to the middle of the political spectrum. The mix of conservatism and liberalism created an interesting dynamic. As an independent voter with a historical footprint of voting across the political spectrum, migrating to an area of Texas with such diverse voting blocks helped me appreciate the state even more.

Another benefit was that Texas is one of the states that does not levy state taxes on individuals, which meant more money in my pocket to manage my expenses or to enjoy discretionary spending. This could also be why it ranks in the top three states with the most billionaires, as well as being home to several industries including energy, technology, and health and wellness. With low taxes, plenty of housing, and full employment, Texas was the biggest hidden gem in plain sight. Its plethora of colleges and universities, quality eateries, and relatively low cost of living (at least by comparison to other larger states, such as California), this was the ideal place for me to start my professional career. In fact, Thomas Sowell notes that in "Houston during the late 1970s, average incomes surged well ahead of the rest of the US, but nevertheless, Houston remained one of the fifteen least expensive housing markets of the 319 US regions examined by Coldwell Banker."

For someone who loves sports, 1995 was an ideal time to move to Houston. The state is home to several different professional sports teams including football, basketball, soccer, and baseball. That year, the Houston Rockets won their second championship, and the whole city was immersed in celebration. Their team had reached the pinnacle of the sport. Back in Louisiana, there were few, if any, sports bars where I wanted to hang out, and not much at the time to celebrate. But I had started out in Houston on a solid foundation. I found myself watching the Rockets advance to conference finals and beyond with my new buddies from work at various sports bars all around the city. The whole experience was something new and very different.

Not to troll the Dallas Cowboys too much, but even they were in the mix for greatness in 1995. The entire state, and in particular the city of Houston, was electric, rowdy, and crowded. It was the perfect time to be right where I was.

IV

EXPERIENCING PROSPERITY, LOSSES, AND GRIT

Being productive will cost you something—
and it will ultimately take you further than any of your perceived limitations.

Study hard, work hard, reap the rewards.

Between the years of 1995 and 2000, I finished up my Master of Business Administration degree, enjoyed full-time employment, got married, watched my daughter grow up to reach nine years old, and experienced the birth of my first son. A lot was happening very fast, and it was indeed stressful. I was pushing myself to breakable limits just to keep up, and my family was conscious of the enormous pressure by extension. Everyone was adjusting, though things were not easy for any of us. My daughter could see it and feel it too. Our relationship was not as harmonious and close as it had been in years prior. Times were tough, but most certainly productive.

Acquiring my MBA was an arduous yet rewarding two-year process. At the time, Shell Oil Company was a people-focused company that, on approval, would pay for advanced degrees. I jumped at the opportunity, and Shell bore the entire cost through a private and respected university in Houston. In many cases, the individuals who pursued post-graduate degrees that Shell Oil Company was paying for had to sign agreements that they would not depart for at least two years. This for me was totally fine. The company was a great place to work and the health benefits were second to none. In my mind, it was all happening within a transactional understanding—meaning, it was intended to have bi-directional benefits. Shell expected me to bring my learnings back to the company to build on their cash position as well as their culture. The benefit for me was that I would be able to expand my knowledge and worldview, as well as my promotional positioning. It was a win-win proposition.

There I was again—back in school, learning about money. I suppose my fascination with money was such that, since I never had a lot of it growing up, once I did acquire it, I wanted to know how to multiply it, enjoy it, and preserve some of it for my children and my children's children. Even so, pursuing my MBA was arduous, as is often the case for advanced degrees. For two years, my routine was to rise at 5:30 in the morning to enter into an hour or more of rush-hour traffic, making my way to our downtown offices by roughly 7:30. I would leave the workplace by 4:45 to attend classes between 5:15 and 8:00. Afterward, I would head to the campus library until 10:00, making my way home by 11:15 or so. After a late snack or meal after a shower, I would be in bed by 12:30 a.m., only to start the process all over again a few hours later. It was well worth it. Because competition was stiff and delivering at a high-performance level was the standard, I can say that acquiring a post-graduate degree gave me a competitive edge when competing for roles and promotions.

The question of a higher education or a specialized skill and which is more important is a common one. I do not see it as a question of which is more important, but rather *both and*. Whilst I am a staunch proponent of higher education, I am just as exuberant about acquiring a specialized skill. First, I will humbly state the obvious: Your education can never be taken away. It is yours. Whilst I did not enjoy school as an adolescent, higher education helped to broaden my myopic thinking. I can remember all the required reading, though I never enjoyed doing it in my early years of school, and I am today a voracious reader. I like the feel and to hear the crispness of the pages turn as I read, looking intently for nuggets of insight to improve my own life. Self-improvement is a lifelong process, and if I desire to grow as a person and increase my knowledge, the $24.99 cost of a book actually represents something priceless. Further, higher education has, at least in part, given me the courage to write *this* book.

Higher education also expands the bounds of a social network and builds the skill of collaborative study. In the world of work, you will be required to work in teams and work on projects that require connecting with other people. Higher education is a launching pad to develop these skills. It can also facilitate the development of lifelong friendships. This social network often leads to opportunities and open doors that would otherwise be closed to you. Importantly, higher education drives the critical thinking skills that are necessary for any career. These skills support you in solving problems using practical logic and creative thinking.

When the opportunity to pursue higher education presents itself, one should grab onto it. Yet, for many years, our society has been driven by capturing that degree under the assumption that it made securing a job achievable. With the advent of technology that moves as fast as it is moving, specialized skills are invaluable. By this, I mean the skills of an electrician, a plumber, a welder, a claims adjuster, a carpenter, a mechanic, and so on. That specialized skill makes room for your family to eat and be taken care of for as long as that product or service is in demand. Developing a specialized skill adjoined to a higher education can keep the reality of poverty at bay and be prosperous.

This two-fold approach comes from textbook knowledge of basic supply and demand. If the product or service you're skilled in is a commodity and the demand is high, and your supply of that product or service is delivered at a quality level, it can lead to your financial elevation.

Hard work is required to get the training to secure a specialized skill. Hard work is involved to search without ceasing to secure the role of an apprentice for that skill. There is hard work to be done, diligently enhancing that specialized skill to the extent that it cannot be ignored. But the same goes for pursuing a higher education. Hard work is required to consistently study and ultimately secure that degree. There is hard work to be done if you are to pursue meaningful work and consistently build a career to the extent that your expertise cannot be ignored.

Study hard, work hard, reap the rewards—these are not throwaway words. They are real. Real in the sense that you get out what you put in. Never stop learning, and never stop earning. That is, never stop diligently pursuing your efforts to manage and maintain a stable financial foundation. This is one of the few life stressors that can be minimized or eliminated based on your decisions.

Money is only a tool;
don't fall in love with it.

People often misunderstand the principle of money. In my view, there is no problem with money, and there is no problem with having lots of it. Money makes room to provide for your children and your children's children. Money makes room for philanthropy and charitable acts of kindness. Money makes room for your enjoyment. Most importantly, money makes room for building the kingdom of God.

However, I must add a word of caution about money. One must be judicious with it, ethical with it, and gracious with it. Otherwise, we set ourselves up for distress and disappointment. Being judicious with money means that it is to be used in a thoughtful way that does not harm others. Being ethical with money means being honest and aligned with one's personal values in our financial dealings. Being gracious with money means being a conscious giver with the aim of making a meaningful difference to causes that matter to you. "For the love of money" (that is, the greedy desire for it and the willingness to gain it unethically) "is a root of all sorts of evil. Some people, eager for money, have wandered from faith and pierced themselves with many griefs." (1 Timothy 6:10). I say, as long as you can be judicious, ethical, and gracious, go out and earn as much money as you can.

Having a specialized skill as well as higher education makes it possible for you to enlarge your territory and make room for a significant financial increase. Going a bit further, the specialized skill in particular makes a pathway to create multiple streams of income. It is the force behind the financial flow into your accounts, like gravity into a lake, river, or ocean. In keeping with the analogy of a live water stream: streams provide an important ecosystem for plants and animals, drinking water and irrigation for crops, electricity through hydropower, and replenishment of groundwater reserves. Generating money and landing multiple streams of income can be similarly beneficial to you, your family, and others.

It is important to remember that, as we pursue various opportunity streams or multiple streams of income, we must keep the main thing the main thing. At any given point in my own journey, I made sure to have three to four streams of income, and as a conscious investor and saver, that extra income became a safety net for a downturn in the economy or a family emergency that might require an outlay of cash. Similarly, in the pursuit of these streams, never, ever lose focus on that which provides your primary source of income. The quality of your work must consistently produce excellence, and this must not be ignored or minimized.

What about the decision to work in corporate America versus that of entrepreneurship? Ultimately, this is dependent upon you and the makeup of your character. Not everyone is cut out for working in corporate America. In many cases, it is structured, formal, hierarchal, performance-based, routine, and deliberate in its strategic outcomes. When you can be diligent at progressing up the corporate ladder, this kind of career does allow you to consistently build wealth over time.

I have worked with many people in corporate America who have retired as multimillionaires. Because their company contributed to their pension and 401k, they made sure to match or exceed that contribution from the company. They were steady, consistent, and deliberate. Then, over years of compound interest, they were able to reap the benefits of financial security.

Entrepreneurship requires drive, ingenuity, creative problem solving, relationship building, and the ability to endure uncertainty. Notwithstanding its challenges, entrepreneurship can be rewarding in so many capacities, especially when your product or service is in demand and you offer it with quality and exceptional skill. Entrepreneurship can also allow one to leave that prized legacy of potential wealth for subsequent generations. Yet just as not everyone can work in the structured corporate environment, not everyone can work in an environment of entrepreneurial uncertainty. You must define which work environment works best for you.

As for me, I chose to focus my primary income stream on corporate America. This decision had primarily centered around the reality that I had a young family to consider, and ensuring I had health benefits to cover them was a priority for me. I remembered what it was like to not have good healthcare benefits as a youngster, having to go to charity hospitals and wait for hours upon hours to be seen by the hospital staff. I could not envisage subjecting my young family to that same fate.

However, whilst I worked in corporate America, for many years I also pierced the veil of entrepreneurship. In 2007, alongside my regular job—keeping the main thing the main thing—I sank my teeth into running a business and being directly responsible for the employment of other people and making sound business decisions to maintain a vibrant business.

Both my pops and my uncle had been seasoned authorities in the trucking and transportation space. Though I had no direct experience in logistics, they both thought I would be a good fit to own a transportation company. First, I explored the idea, peppered them both with hundreds of questions, and conducted deep dive research to understand how this type of business worked. Then, after a few months of due diligence and securing all the federal and state licenses and certifications, I filed for incorporation of the business. After that, I moved fast. I partnered with a young man who had his own trucking authority; he handled operations, and I handled the business administration side. A few years later, I launched out independently and amassed several 18-wheelers (some of which belonged to independent operators that were leased to my company), several local transport units, and other accessories and equipment. Over time, my company grew large enough to hire a couple of salespeople, an office manager, and a dispatcher.

The key to doing all of this while maintaining my corporate job was to find the best transportation industry expert I could find. He was the absolute best in the business, with over twenty years of experience. I hired him as the Chief Operating Officer of my company, and his job was to oversee all operations including the drivers, sales staff, dispatchers, and administration office. Next, I personally developed templates, tools, and programs for the staff to use as guidelines for decision making, safety protocols, and all expenditures. Once the staff was sufficiently in place and their guidelines were established,

I simply ran a nose-in, hands-off business model that allowed me to focus on my corporate job during the day.

After I left my corporate job in the evening, I would make the trek over to our offices to review the operational reports, financial reports, and key performance indicators I had developed. Whilst my primary role was to get out of the way and let the best of the best do what they do, I did personally manage the cashflow, including invoicing and any debt collections. This taught me the nuances of conducting "start-up" operations for a new business, the direct application of capital allocation, and the impact finances have on business survival. I also learned sales strategies and the deeper relational and emotional intelligence aspects of ensuring that the people working for my company were able to put food on their tables.

After several years of owning the business, my company had cumulatively generated millions in revenue over the course of some years. This also meant I had begun to experience the impacts of increasing governmental regulation, finding qualified truck drivers, and increasing marital challenges that required my attention. So, I sold the business. But by then, I knew my way around the corporate ecosystem and had taught myself entrepreneurship from the grassroots level. I had grown a startup into a proficient and thriving small business.

There are various legitimate routes to earn money, so I recommend you find your lane and move forward within it. No matter what, work to develop skills and expertise that can meet the demands of the market. Your legacy, if this is important to you, just might depend on it.

My first day at Shell Oil Company was June 19, 1995, starting out as a Distribution Coordinator with the responsibility of trading and scheduling Liquid Propane Gas (LPG) via rail throughout the continental USA. I took pride in my work, and this was reflected in the longevity of productivity. My time with Shell ultimately spanned almost three decades.

That is right, yes—I started my first day of corporate life on the day recognized as "Juneteenth." On June 19, 1865, Union Major-General Gordon Granger in Galveston, Texas, issued the military order to free slaves. In accordance with a proclamation from the executive of the United States, all slaves were free. Abraham Lincoln had presented the Emancipation Proclamation two years earlier in 1863, declaring freedom for enslaved people in the Confederate states. It took two more years for the 13th Amendment to the United States Constitution to provide that "neither slavery nor involuntary servitude, except as a punishment for crime whereof the party shall have been duly convicted, shall exist within the United States, or any place subject to their jurisdiction." However, the news did not reach the enslaved people in Texas until months after the ratification of that amendment.

When I walked the halls of Shell Oil Company in my white, crisp shirts and tailored, pressed slacks—outfitted with a brand-new pager provided by the company—I remember feeling as if I had been freed from the enslaved grips of public housing. This was the best job I could have asked for on the launching pad straight out of college. Our team of Distribution Coordinators/Gas Traders was consistently on call to handle delays or any public catastrophes in addition to our daily role of moving gas throughout the continental US. It was all very exciting, moving and redirecting gas, negotiating and surveilling gas prices, and monitoring indexes. It could also be a bit overwhelming.

I was working alongside two very experienced female gas traders who had both been in the business for a while. They were smart, shrewd, and savvy. Meanwhile, I had very little on-the-job training coming out of college, so I made my share of errors and flawed judgment calls. I didn't know what I didn't know. And I did not know a thing about office politics. For example, I spoke to and had lunch with people no matter their role in the company. It did not matter to me if they worked in the mailroom, the cafeteria, or wherever. Unfortunately, I learned that working in the trading team meant being a part of an exclusive community. Fraternizing across the company made me more of an outsider working in the gas trading team, and there were times I felt unwelcomed as a result.

An especially difficult lesson came through one of the senior managers from another department, who I supposed I had a good relationship with. That is, until he felt comfortable enough with me to make a very off-colored, backhanded joke. At least, I took it as if he was making a joke that I did not find funny at all: "Carnell, what do you need that pager for, your drug deals?"

My first instinct was to reach back to the days of old and slap the heck out of him, followed up with a few expletives outlining my insistence that I was not to be spoken to in that manner. Given I had matured just a little bit, I was able to gather myself and count the cost of my reaction, then simply say, "I do not sell drugs, and I have never sold drugs. If you are looking for drugs, you are speaking to the wrong guy."

Once again, I was a young lad, and I really didn't know much about the corporate world I'd found myself in. Fresh out of college and just eight months into corporate life, I had quickly learned that you can never be too friendly with people in the workplace, lest you open the door for judgment and disrespect. Share and engage only enough to build camaraderie and good team dynamics, but never share so much that you and your personal life are on the agenda for meetings or hall talk that you are not invited to.

"We are free only insofar as we exercise control over what people know about us, and in what circumstances they come to know it."[11]

As a new hire in the company, I was in the job rotational program, which allowed new hires out of college to spend 12–18 months in a role, rotating over a total period of three to four years across various parts of the business. The idea was to create exposure to different parts of the business as fast as possible. This was, in my view, a brilliant introduction to the business. I spent 18 months in the Distribution Coordinator/Gas Trader role before being shifted to the treasury department and a role that put me in the thick of finance and accounting for a number of Shell Oil Company's small business investments in joint ventures.

The treasury role was based on the 46th floor of a high-rise corporate building overlooking the downtown Houston skyline. By this point, I had started to deeply internalize the benefits of healthy diversity and inclusion. During those years, the leadership at Shell Oil Company were conscientious about ensuring opportunities were available for People of Color and for women. Whilst progress was slow and, at times, delayed, I at least appreciated the effort the company was making. I counted my blessings that someone who looked like me could work in an environment that did not look like me. I had earned my opportunity, but because the people who did not look like me had the power to say yay or nay to my employment—to my ability to earn a living—that opportunity would not have been available without an inclusion program.

I would often pinch myself. How could a young lad from the big yellow apartments make his way to corporate life, landing in a high-rise corporate building? Now, I would say it was the hand of God, followed by living in the greatest country in the world, these United States of America. For all its challenges and issues, and notwithstanding the way politics can drive a nation toward progression or regression, the United States makes room for real "rags to relevant" stories. I can acknowledge living in the greatest country in the world while at the same time acknowledging that the United States has a long way to go toward a more perfect union. If we are to become an absolute color-blind society and to continue to make this the greatest country in the world, we all have an individual part to play.

One simple but nuanced, layered principle we can all follow is merely to treat others as you would wish to be treated—regardless of color. I say nuanced and layered to avoid being overly simplistic about this topic, because I do realize that much of American history has not been resolved or even discussed with full transparency, frankness, and honesty among the races. Hence, I say once more, we all individually have a part to play if we are to uphold the ideals of a more perfect union.

I was working in this high rise on the morning of September 11, 2001—a terrifying time for anyone in the country working in a downtown locale. That morning, I had followed my routine of waking at 5:30 a.m. and making my way to the office by roughly 7:30. As we all now know, it was anything but a normal day. Before I could make my way to the underground tunnels to grab a quick breakfast sandwich, every television in the building echoed with the heart-stopping words, "There is breaking news."

Everyone in my office was diverted from their work, standing in front of wall-mounted televisions as reports relayed as much real-time information as they could. War had been initiated against the United States. It was not a traditional war, with artillery and boots on the ground, your men and women against my men and women. No, it was not that. The ideology of terror had taken center stage for the entire world to witness.

We would all come to learn that nineteen individuals had committed a heinous act of terror, hijacking commercial airliners and crashing them into the Twin Towers of the World Trade Center in New York City as well as the Pentagon (headquarters of the US Department of Defense). A fourth plane was hijacked as well, but the passengers revolted and crashed it into a field in rural Pennsylvania. This atrocity occurred on so many levels of America's way of life, taking full advantage of the ideology of terror.

This was one of the deadliest attacks in American history.[12] This galvanized the US government and citizens in a way that I had never seen in my lifetime. The American citizens were in full support of the US government seeking justice—and rightfully so. On this occasion, it was the color of justice rather than the color of our skin that ruled the day.

*Competent, thoughtful diversity in the
workplace makes space for fruitful
growth and an edge over the competition.*

Shortly after the horrific attack on September 11, 2001, my next rotation began, and I became a business analyst in the innovation and research side of the business. In this role, I oversaw the financial analysis for over thirty million dollars in revenue, generated by ten different business units. I was joined by three other business analysts supporting other units, and each of them came from different backgrounds and cultures than me. In our team of four alone, there were four different countries represented—the United States, the United Kingdom, India, and China. This diversity enabled creative thinking, created rich and healthy competition between us, and in the end, developed lifelong friendships.

Whilst each of us on this unlikely team of two women and two men with vast cultural differences had our own way of doing the work, we also collaborated and shared ideas amongst ourselves. We checked our egos at the door and thus discovered creative ways to solve problems. This brought the entire team accolades from around the department, as our work was instrumental in the financial growth of the entire organization.

Here is what I learned from working with this diverse team of healthy rivals, each supporting our respective departments: diversity led to a multiplicity of ideas, a multiplicity of individual and team-wide growth, and a multiplicity of creative perspectives. In other words, everything was multiplied, thereby unlocking significant economic value to the organization. By the end of my tenure as a business analyst, my responsibility for financial analysis had grown to more than one hundred million dollars in revenue, and our team of colleagues had turned into dear friendships that would carry forward for more than two decades.

We often invited each other over to our homes for meals that represented our respective countries. We also bonded around the antics of our line manager at the time—a big, burly White guy named Bill. He was a no-nonsense straight shooter, with commentary that was sometimes peppered with colorful and humorous anecdotes about anyone who had taken a position against him or any of his decisions. He was also a prankster, and if he did not like you, you knew it immediately. At the same time, Bill was well-regarded in the organization, even with his brashness. If you reported to Bill, you knew he had you covered like an umbrella from the rain of internal politics. For those of us who were not at the table when human resources were being discussed, we could rest knowing he was speaking on our behalf as our fearless leader. As I have had time to reflect, in all of my career, there have been very few leaders or managers who could both lead people effectively and be competent technically. Yet Bill met that criteria, and I was grateful to have met him within five to six years of employment with Shell Oil Company.

You had to have thick skin working with Bill, and I had a solid working relationship with him. Once, with a deadline to meet, I was tasked with developing the messaging package, including financials, to present to senior management. I double- and triple-checked the package before submitting to Bill for review. He was in my office immediately, saying, "Carnell, you screwed this report up." (Actually, he did not use the word "screwed." He used one of his classic, humorous phrases.) With somewhat of a smirk on my face, I told him it was a matter of perspective, but that I would update the report and get it back to him within the hour. I knew not to overreact or take it personally. I sent the report back to Bill within the hour as I said I would, then he looked it over and said, "Good job, let's do lunch sometime this week."

When it was time for performance discussions, I had expected a backlash for the few times he and I held different perspectives about getting things done. But no, it was not the case. After reporting to Bill for just over a year, I was given my highest performance rating to that point at Shell Oil Company. Bill recognized the long hours I had put in, the positive feedback from my stakeholders, and my zeal and willingness to learn. Bill never mentioned us not seeing eye-to-eye. His position was that we would not always agree, but we could discuss, align, and move on. Case closed!

My all-time greatest encounter with Bill occurred one early Tuesday morning. Arriving to the office early as usual, with my crisp white shirt and tailored, pressed slacks, I saw Bill coming towards me in the hallway. Before I could even greet him, he said, "Moses, have you been to Europe yet?" We were headquartered in The Netherlands at the time, but I hadn't been any further away from the country than a couple of trips to the Caribbean islands. When I said no, he smiled a bit sheepishly and said, "I know you just made it to the office, but I want you to go home now and pack your stuff." (Of course, he did not use the word *stuff*.) "You and I are leaving for The Netherlands tomorrow morning."

Still a novice in the corporate world and not yet exposed to any world outside of the United States, I was a fish out of water. It was all so far beyond my upbringing in public housing. I did not know a thing about corporate travel, not to mention flying business class. Hence, I arrived at the airport the next morning with the biggest suitcase in tow—for a three-day trip. Again, I knew nothing. Later, Bill taught me how to roll my clothes tightly a certain way and pack them in a specific way to maximize the volume of clothing in a carry-on travel bag for ease of boarding and deplaning and easy maneuvering in and out of the airport for a short business trip.

After flying through the night, stretching enough to be comfortable in our fully reclining business class seats, we touched down at Amsterdam Airport Schiphol (AMS). We had enjoyed a steak dinner on the plane the night before and awoke to our breakfast of choice, paired with a warm towel to refresh from the overnight haul. Then we took a private car to our hotel and went to our respective rooms for a quick refreshing shower before heading straight to the office for a full day's work starting at 7:30 a.m. This was interesting to me, because he and I were the only two in the office. The European staff did not get started until roughly 9:00 a.m.

This experience set me up for a subsequent role that required me to travel throughout Europe, South America, and the Far East. In short, Bill had exposed me to a whole new world.

During my three decades with Shell Oil Company, Bill was the only senior leader (who I worked with, anyway) who would invite his entire staff over to his home during Christmastime. All other leaders would host departmental Christmas parties at restaurants, but he was just that open and personable. Bill was the primary catalyst for my corporate growth and my sponsor who supported me through my next few roles in Shell Oil Company. When I eventually got word of his passing, there was no way I would miss his funeral services. To Bill, I am eternally grateful.

My next role, that of a Corporate Auditor, required me to travel at least twenty to thirty percent of the time. Company policy directed that if any air travel was longer than so many hours, that employee would need to travel business class for personal safety reasons. This put my corporate travel in business class. Thanks to Bill, I knew what to expect and how to handle the opportunity presented to me. I learned to travel as if I belonged there. Me and my auditing colleagues would fly to our respective destinations, handle our professional business, then enjoy cultural meals and do some sight-seeing as time permitted. We would maintain a non-residential presence in these countries for three to four weeks at a time, opening my lens of exposure to other countries and cultures wider than I could have imagined.

There were also some vexatious experiences, like having traveled to Rotterdam in January for an audit. We were snowed in and worked from the hotel for a couple of weeks, with no opportunity to sight-see or enjoy the city. On another occasion, I remember traveling to The Netherlands for an audit, only to find that all the documents we had requested for review came back to us in Dutch—notwithstanding the agreement that all documents requested would be in English. My colleague and I made the best of it, becoming Google experts along the way. We spent large amounts of time converting the language so that we could review and report accordingly. It was no easy task, but we accomplished our goal and finished the audit.

After finishing our work wherever in the world we might be, we would hop back on a five-to-seventeen-hour return flight to the United States, once again enjoying a nice meal (most of the time it was a steak for me) and a choice of wine or cocktail. My appreciation for different countries, food choices, governmental operations, living conditions, and driving habits—to name only a few of the differences these trips exposed me to—led me to a whole new level of personal growth. My perspective widened, and my level of respect for different cultures and countries was elevated.

This global exposure also took me to new heights in directly working with and coming to understand people of different cultures. In the auditing world, especially in a global company, most of the audits were comprised of employees from around the world. If you were assigned to an audit in a different country, you were most likely to meet your audit-mates for the first time upon your arrival, and they were likely a team with mixed representation from various different countries.

Just after Hurricane Katrina ravaged the Gulf Coast and Louisiana in particular, I was assigned to an audit in Singapore, then was joined by colleagues who were Omani. I remember that we were sitting in the forecourt of a restaurant when my colleague from Oman asked, "What happened in New Orleans? With all the displaced people?" He had read an article about the working poor in New Orleans and was genuinely shocked and dismayed. Not only for the loss of life and property, but because he had never been to the United States and had previously believed that everyone, including People of Color, were rich.

Once again, I learned that exposure to different things, different people, and different cultures is a gift, allowing us to understand the fragile nature of humanity, in all its complicated forms.

My next role thrust me into the world of leadership. I learned quickly that relating to and leading people, regardless of their position or title, is a demonstration of both humility and courage. It is not a foregone conclusion that all leaders have the presence of mind to do this. Looking beyond titles and positions, especially in a politically charged environment that is cemented in territorial positioning and upward progression, is not easy. Managing up the organization and leading down the organization requires integrity and a great deal of love for people.

As a new leader in our Commercial Fuels organization, my focus was on my first one hundred days in the role. This, in part, encompassed meeting the other leaders within my department, meeting my direct reports who were engaged on the front lines, understanding and refreshing my team strategy, and developing a list of immediate priorities that were considered low-hanging fruit. I had learned from my audit days that it was perfectly fine to request an informal audit of the work that the teams I would lead had done, to more clearly understand any risks we faced from the outset. This allowed me, as the new leader, to identify our larger issues and quickly put a plan in place to mitigate any open exposure.

So there I was, off and running with my new team, making immediate, meaningful, and impactful changes in both the short and long term. Almost immediately, I discovered that the organization was devoid of any sort of system that could provide transparent data on the true profitability of our sales contracts. This lack of visibility exposed the organization to the potential for misleading financial reporting. After several rounds of meetings with the leadership of the organization and employees working on the front lines, I pulled a team together to roll out a system to address the issue. Only, no one was willing to expend their political capital to get the issue resolved. No one wanted to risk their reputation to try to solve the issue, in the instance that it might fail and thereby limit their upward mobility. In fact, my understanding was that the issue had lingered for a long period of time with no one willing to articulate it to the executive leadership.

Enter me, with a temperament that leans into difficult situations with little regard for commendations. My mindset, my instincts, and my very nature does not operate well in an environment of unresolved chaos. Instinctively, I look for opportunities to resolve or simplify the complexity. So my team and I rolled out a department-wide plan. Within eight months, we were on track to deliver one of the biggest, most successful system rollouts in organizational history.

Later, as a result of internal merging and my growing influence in the organization, I led an even larger operations team, which grew to as many as twenty direct reports in a very short period of time. My leadership style continued to get noticed and gain traction in the organization, which led to my candidacy for more senior-level positions down the line.

In a very unique way, my maneuvering in public housing had prepared me for the rough game of corporate politics. I had developed the skills to observe and listen carefully to both what was being said *and* what was being inferred. I learned to quickly address issues or to make the calculated decision to ignore certain situations that did not deserve my attention. Given my upbringing, facing difficult decisions and leaning into difficult situations had become part of my DNA, and this led to my success as a leader in the corporate world.

The concept of leadership that follows is truly the culmination of many years of observation and experience. I saw people who had been placed in leadership roles but avoided difficult situations or discussions. I saw some who intentionally stoked chaos. Others were only interested in their own upward progression. On a few occasions, I witnessed the virtues of great leadership in those who favored what was right versus who was right. They didn't shy away from difficult situations, and whilst they praised individuals and teams for a job well done, they never sought to take full credit. They pushed their teams forward to achieve greatness, through the qualities I have outlined as LEADER: Listening, Empathy, Awareness, Discipline, Empowerment, and Resiliency.

Believe it or not, listening is a skill—and it is hard. When we engage in a conversation, how many of us drift off, perhaps thinking about the next thing we want to say in the discussion? This also includes looking to solve the issue whilst engaged in a discussion. It happens all the time.

I worked extremely hard to develop a rapport with everyone who worked in the teams I led. For example, I would engage in real-time performance discussions that gave feedback that would allow the employees to grow. I had always thought it was wrong to document people's missteps and then wait until the end-of-the-year performance review to let the individual know about missteps that occurred many months prior. Unfortunately, those kinds of office politics games were played all the time, and it became even worse as I progressed up the corporate ladder.

I remember trying to get my arms around the details of a four-hundred-plus page, ongoing and incomplete contract that I did not negotiate, and for which the line manager who was negotiating it would not share supporting documents. Because I engaged with the suppliers while referencing the contract as part of my role, there could be no movement without understanding those supporting contents, which continued to be held by that line manager. This was a calculated move on her part, so as to be looked upon as the only knowledgeable person at the table.

It was not a pleasant experience, but the order of the day was to thoroughly understand that four-hundred-page contract. So, each time the line manager spoke about the supporting documents, I took copious notes, ultimately accumulating a catalog of supporting content. Over time, I became armed with all the information I needed to effectively collaborate and negotiate with the supplier myself. Later, when I moved on to a new role, it was easy for me to leave a knowledge path for my successor.

The key for success in this situation was listening to the line manager and taking appropriate notes. Listening to suppliers, listening to leadership, and listening to colleagues—lots of listening all culminated to getting that contract completed and signed before I transitioned to another role.

During my time as a leader of teams, I would like to think that I coined the terminology of "skip-level" meetings within the company. At the time I was using this terminology—roughly 2009—I do not remember it being a thing anywhere else. Nevertheless, a few times a year I engaged in one-to-one meetings with the folks who were on the front lines, skipping the supervisors and managers who were reporting directly to me. This gave me the opportunity to listen to what my team was doing well and what we could improve on, directly from the people who were affected by our decisions.

In skip-level meetings, people were free to talk about the good and the bad, though we did not try to solve problems and we did not allow any talk about other people—that is, no tittle-tattling. I listened, gathering intelligence and feedback to drive best practices in the team. Most importantly, these skip-level meetings allowed me to get to know each of my team members on a personal level. Because these discussions were not transactional, by simply taking time to listen, I found that people will share what they value. When we take time to listen and engage, we can find that center point of value and then use it to help each other grow.

Empathy

Coming from public housing granted me the ability to process things from another person's perspective and to understand the emotions behind an action. It was and is something of an effortless skill for me, in the sense that I understood from my very own experiences of destitute and difficult situations that no one is exempt from difficulty. From this level of personal understanding, I could easily find empathy for others, even at a very young age.

When I got to the leadership table, I became privy to the closed-door annual performance discussions for all the employees in the organization. At one point, a Black lady who did not work in my team had been perceived as brash and direct. I also knew, from working on a few projects with her, that she was extremely competent. She simply had a direct, no-nonsense personality. Working with her, you had to know your stuff, as she would hold any and everyone accountable.

During the end-of-year performance review time, I was the only Black leader at that leadership table, alongside six other leaders who were all White men. When it was time to discuss her performance, one of the managers said, "She has delivered on her metrics, but I have to give a low ranking because she has a bad attitude."

Even though she did not report to me, I had to respond. In a poised, diplomatic fashion, seasoned with courage, conviction, and empathy, I looked around the table and posed a few questions that would politely challenge this narrative. Did she deliver on her metrics? Did anyone from this leadership team give her real-time feedback? Did she make good decisions when it came to the bottom line and saving the organization money? Did she work hard?

"Given the answers to these questions," I concluded, "How in good conscience do we give her a low ranking?" I suggested we give her real-time feedback and perhaps provide her with a coach or mentor, while recognizing her contributions to the organization for their critical, if thankless, importance to the organization. In the end, thanks to a bit of empathy for her being misunderstood, she received a ranking much higher than what was initially put on the table.

It is lazy leadership to take a few anecdotes and develop a narrative rather than doing the real work of understanding. After all, the same manager who had made those comments about the lady had been known as a pernicious and bombastic personality type. He had ascended the ranks for his abilities to manage upward well and present materials well. Otherwise, it was well-known that he was bankrupt in empathy—and at leading people, for that matter.

Much later, I went on to support and recommend that lady for a leadership role much like the one I had held many years prior. She was awarded the promotion.

Developing and maintaining an astute sense of self-awareness is a critical component to every aspect of life. No one should know you better than you. What are your likes and dislikes? Are you an introvert, an extrovert, or an ambivert? Do you enjoy social settings? Are you a left-brained person functioning in logic and analytical thinking, or are you a right-brained person moving in the creative and artistic space? Are you a minimalist or a hoarder? Do you enjoy the outdoors or prefer to be indoors? Knowing who you are as a person is crucial to understanding who you are as a leader.

Don Clifton is known as the father of strengths psychology and inventor of the CliftonStrengths assessment to identify a person's personal strengths.[13] When I took the test, it confirmed what I already knew about myself. I have a strong "responsibility" theme that forces me to take psychological ownership for anything I commit to; large or small, I am bound to follow it through to completion. The test also indicated an "intellectual" theme. Meaning, I like mental activity and am very much an introspective person. As an ambivert, I can function in a social setting, but I need alone time and can be my own best companion.

The test also verified that I have a constant need for achievement. I have an internal fire burning inside me that pushes me to do more and achieve more. I also have an "analytical" theme. I like data, and apart from it, I am objective and dispassionate, with no personal agenda. Show me data; prove it. This challenges other people. Lastly, the test validated that I have a "strategic" theme that enables me to sort through the clutter and find the best route. The more complex an issue, the more my mind executes its own interesting, strategic phenomenon to simplify the complexity. The test itself notes that this is not a skill that can be taught; it is a distinct way of thinking, a special perspective on the world at large, where I can see patterns in places others simply see complexity.

Whilst I have certainly made my share of mistakes, for reasons I cannot explain, I have always operated by a strong internal code of right and wrong. If I take a minute to think deeply, I believe the lineage of Moses men who preceded me, in many cases, carried themselves just the same. With this self-awareness, office politics often grated against this internal code. I could tell early that this way of functioning would not play well within a corporate environment. Yet I was self-aware enough to know and accept that not playing along could be a career-limiting mistake. I reminded myself that working in corporate America was a means to an end. I had a young family to take care of, and entrepreneurship was not an immediate option, so I had to find my way through.

Early in my career, I recall one particularly introspective flight to Singapore. Reclined and drifting off to sleep, I prayed to God, declaring that I would be absolutely exultant if I were blessed with a role at a certain level in the company. Just be careful what you ask for, because you just might get it—and only it. I retired from Shell Oil Company at the level I had prayed for many years prior, high enough in the company to be afforded the opportunity to lead teams while earning a significant base salary and stock options as well. But because I never played into the game of office politics well, there was no upward mobility beyond what I had prayed for all those years ago.

I do not regret this. Overall, Shell Oil Company was a great company to make into a full career. The culture provided an astounding place to learn, grow, and make a living. But if promotion and progression meant adversely impacting people, I did not want those promotions. Because of this, I was often labeled as difficult to work with, and I was even subject to ridicule in some cases. Once again, being self-aware, I was completely accepting of these pernicious labels. The end justified the means.

I was willing to walk through this fire for three reasons: to provide for my family; to make the world a better place, sustained with the energy it needs; and to remain long enough to earn a fully funded retirement plan. I made a commitment to that outcome, put in the work, and lasted three decades.

This is me. So, who are you?

Discipline, to me, is a state of mind. It drives the will to consistently offer the best of yourself, regardless of the task or issue. This was my perspective when playing competitive sports during my youth and working in corporate America into my adult years. From competing for Presidential Physical Fitness awards to the basketball court to foot races with my young friends, or eventually supporting my company's drive to be in the top quartile in the industry—it all required discipline. Over the years, as I intently observed other strong leaders alongside my own bag of near-militaristic behaviors, five key habits of a disciplined man emerged.

First, he is consistent. Everyone is accountable to someone. Great employers and entrepreneurs are keenly aware that if their product or service is not consistently delivered to meet that accountability, they have no business. If you are expected to routinely provide a specific product or service, you must challenge yourself to meet that level of expectation. Your role as a leader is to demonstrate a model of consistency; your brand as a leader must be one of consistency. This is the key to breakthrough. Regardless of the task, be it big or small, do it consistently or not at all.

Next, he honors his commitments. When you commit to something, do it to the best of your ability—no excuses. Excuses are an empty jar of nothingness, and who wants to work with someone who turns up empty jars? Doing what you say you will do puts your credibility at stake. It defines who you are. Employers and entrepreneurs justifiably want to know if they can count on you. Offering up excuses instead of honoring the commitment leads to a loss of your credibility or at minimum, a fast exit out the door.

Third, he values time as a commodity. Great leaders are efficient and productive. They realize that there are only so many hours in a day to achieve results. These leaders are not *on* time, but rather *ahead of* time. Being fashionably late because you subscribe to some backward law of power, or for any other reason, is unacceptable. Think about it: would you want someone to waste (steal) your time? No well-balanced person would answer "yes" to that question. Wasting time is a crime, figuratively speaking.

Fourth, he takes pride in accomplishments. Leaders set goals for themselves, and they expect to achieve them. Each goal brings a leader closer to making his own desired impact in the world. Whether the goal is big or small, leaders take pride in accomplishing them all.

Lastly, he has a mindset for continuous learning. Great leaders are well read and often capture new learnings for their personal tool kit. They are curious, seeking to understand other perspectives rather than pressing to be understood. Great leaders are also keen to share their knowledge, hoping to see the advancement of others. This innate hunger for knowledge keeps a leader sharp and always ready to be tapped as a resource for good.

In the workplace—or any place, for that matter—no one person can do it all. When we empower people to make certain decisions or to move in a certain direction, we give them the room to grow and develop. As their maturity level elevates, they become a self-sustaining individual in their own right.

I had to trust my team, as well as each individual on their own, to deliver on their assignments. Likewise, the employees had to trust me to set the vision and deliver on that vision. This made hiring critical, so I hired for attitude and aptitude. In other words, I wanted to know whether the potential employee had an attitude that would fit our culture. Secondly, I looked for the aptitude to learn and understand the rigors of the job. Establishing trust was the next most important element. Depending on the role, having previous experience was less important for me.

The leadership I was reporting to at the time had empowered me to lead my team through the delivery of a brand-new, multimillion-dollar logistics system, even though it had not been in my initial slate of responsibilities. They knew and understood that this opportunity to deliver this new logistics system would broaden my skill set and assist with my continued growth and development. So, I did the same for the individuals who worked in my team. I assessed each of their performances and capabilities and assigned broadening deliverables for their continued growth and development. Then I held short, weekly "stand-up" meetings with supervisors to chat about three things: our wins from the previous week, any significant barriers in delivering our work for the upcoming week, and deliverables against our team goals. That was it.

Since I trusted who I had hired, I could also empower them and give them the space to perform. If the employees that I had inherited did not subscribe to the culture or agree with what we were trying to accomplish, they were provided with assistance to move to other teams. The culture was just that important. A culture empowered to deliver and perform. Full stop.

Throughout my nearly three decades in corporate America, I have reported to some great leaders, and I have reported to some less-than-stellar managers. At times, my perspective for the way a strategy should have been documented, approved, and delivered varied widely from the senior manager(s).

On one such occasion, a senior manager tore into my reputation after our very different perspectives for strategy and delivery came to a head. Afterward, it took a very long time to recover my reputation. I also worked with a senior supply chain manager from our operations in another country who made being on her team one of the most challenging working experiences that I and others ever had in the workplace. The level of cultural vitriol and maliciousness sown in that team, as well as the divisiveness sown with our construction and supply partners, was so substantial that when there was a reorganization in the project, her team was restructured and she was moved out of that senior-level role at the time. Notwithstanding, she was given another shot and moved to an individual contributor role. (This was the same manager I referred to earlier, who hoarded information regarding the four hundred page contract.)

I outline these experiences as examples of resilience, since I was able to find my way through. I recovered my reputation, I made it through the difficult environment, and I negotiated and completed a complex and difficult agreement in spite of the distraction she created.

By contrast, I also had the great fortune to work with great leaders—namely, Gosia, Bill, Eric, Wybe, and David. These were brilliant, competent, and people-savvy leaders who understood how to tap into and demonstrate high emotional intelligence. Disagreements will occur in any work environment; however, it is incumbent on you to keep the mission and vision in sight. Be relentless and resilient enough to not get sidetracked and lose focus, no matter what comes your way.

With a bit of self-deprecation, I must admit that I have not always succeeded in every aspect of a job or role. I have bombed a few presentations, usually by overestimating my preparation. However, I was resilient enough to bounce back. I leveraged what could have been career-limiting experiences and learned from them all.

During my last few roles in the company, I managed to negotiate deals valued at more than $250 million in both brownfield and greenfield markets, across the Far East, Europe, South America, and North America. This could only be done with distinct and noticeable attention to detail, alongside the drive to produce more and better results. As I have expressed, I have the unique ability to see patterns and cut through complexity. This quality, plus an uncompromising drive for execution and strategic thinking, allowed me to deliver premium solutions and landmark energy deals. My last senior line leader—a great leader in her own right—saw value in me and my work product and bestowed the highest of commendations for a job well done. To Gosia, I am grateful. I lay all this out to say that there will be ups and downs, peaks, and valleys. If your means justify your end, then demonstrate resiliency and stay the course.

Whilst I do not know *how* one can find resilience—everyone has their own way of defining and handling it—I will say that building resilience is much like building muscle memory. As you encounter roadblocks and setbacks, you must keep pushing through to become stronger at managing challenges until the desired results are achieved.

*"If you fall to pieces in a crisis, there
wasn't much to you in the first place."
(Proverbs 24:10)*

I mentioned earlier that the years between 1995 and 2000 were busy and productive, to include getting married. Then I was blessed with the birth of my first son in the early 2000s, and just four years later, my second son followed. To get straight to the basis of this segment, after fifteen years of marriage, as it was for my mother and my pops some forty years earlier, so it was for me. I too would become a divorcee. The road to different endpoints may be the same at times, but inevitably there will come a point in your journey when the pathways split and you have to choose one way or the other.[14]

I kept my mouth quiet about my divorce. I did not mention one word of it on social media or anywhere else—only to be met with mountains of speculation and ridicule. The arrows were flying from all directions. The Moses name that I had tried to build and protect over so many years became damaged within a couple of months. The center of this crisis for me was the disbandment of our family and the loss daily connection from my children that resulted.

The pain of this experience was only surpassed seven years later, when I lost my mother to lung disease. My mother—the woman who loved me unconditionally. The woman who single-handedly raised my sister and me. The woman who would sacrifice everything for me, who deferred to me for all her big life decisions, who kept food in my belly even during the most meager times. The woman who protected me at any cost.

My mother was gone.

"Pain exists to promote evolution; its cumulative effect finally forces us in a new direction, though the mechanism may be very slow."[15]

The pain from my mother's passing was indescribable. What is it about storms that makes us question God's love? Yet throughout these crises and losses, I realized I had to give God more mental real estate than I had previously allotted. I had to lean on my favorite verse in the Bible: "Be still and know that I am God; I will be exalted among the nations, I will be exalted in the earth." (Psalms 46:10)

You must understand that being still does not mean being stagnant. Stillness is not lost or incapable of seeing things clearly enough to make good decisions. Rather, intentional stillness leads to the mental clarity required to make sound decisions. I realized I could not let the stronghold of crises and losses take me captive in my mind. I knew I could not afford to fall into unwise thinking, so I reconnected with my gift of ignoring all the noise. The core of my strength was best expressed in my very own stillness.

When the storms in our lives are raging and the seas are roaring, that is not the time to make irrational decisions. This is the time to be deliberate and measured and, in some cases, absolutely still. This is the time one can truly hear God—and we must, before we take any further steps.

I remained single for many years after my divorce. In that time, I committed to refocusing and redefining my purpose. And so, not long after she appeared when I least expected it.

I had not planned on going anywhere the evening that I met her, but a friend was convincing enough to get me out of my house. The plan had been to spend a nice, quiet evening at home watching sports. Instead, I found myself at an uptown restaurant with a reformulated plan for fellowship with friends. That's when I saw her across the way, and eventually struck up a conversation.

She was elegant. She was soft spoken. She was stylish. She was graceful. She was educated. She had loving tendencies. She was gorgeous.

She was a gem I could not pass up. Yet because of my own stubborn commitment to refocus and redefine my purpose, we lost touch for several months. Thankfully, we reconnected, and a few years later, I married that gorgeous woman from across the way.

You see, God knows what we need and when we need it, even though we must open our mouths to express our desires. Whenever I prayed for exactly what I wanted, I got exactly what I wanted. When I was still, God gave me what I needed. Finding that sweet spot of alignment is not always easy; it takes work and patience. Yet the rewards, when they arrive, are sweet.

What do you say to two young boys who will see the best side of God's love as well as the dark side of humankind? No matter what they hear from society, in all things and all decisions, man to son, you tell them to err on the side of love.

What is love? Love is one of the strongest forces on earth. Love is thoughtful, love is considerate, love is corrective, love makes provision, love is covering. Love is sacrificial. Love is "choosing to," not "having to."

Now, love does not mean being taken advantage of. Asking God for wisdom and prudence is a wise practice in this regard. To my sons and daughter, this means you must hold firm to your value system and your God-inspired decisions without compromise, even when society tells you something to the contrary.

As a man to his sons, I am steadfast in praying for my sons to err on the side of love each and every day. Further, I ask the Lord to give all fathers more ministry for Him—to enlarge the borders for our sons and daughters and for our children's children as well.[16] For every son needs their father or a father-like figure to say "I love you," and to guide, advise, and correct them along their way. Otherwise, as young boys and as men we have the ability and the propensity to become unwise, unruly human beings, defaulting to animalistic behaviors.

As fathers, we must consider three ways we can make an imprint on our sons:

1. Keep open doors.
2. Coach and teach, not preach.
3. Introduce, inform, and inspire.

The doors of communication must always remain open. Our young boys must feel safe discussing their mistakes, shortcomings, and successes. They must feel safe from the spirit of judgment and overreactions that we as fathers have the proclivity to exhibit. Then, when our young boys feel safe to walk through that open door of communication, this becomes the space and time to listen and guide.

Secondly, let's be real. How many times did we loathe the idea of someone preaching at us as we were youngsters? Especially when the person doing the preaching was no better off at decision making. As fathers, we must coach and teach our sons rather than preaching to them. We must impart nuggets of knowledge and wisdom to our sons, then move on.

When my children come to me, even as they are adults now, I don't look to solve their problems but rather to give them situations and scenarios to consider and think through for themselves. Rather than stating what our sons must do or ought to do, let's challenge our own vernacular, tenor, and tone. Let's suggest to them what they "might consider" as they are making certain decisions, rather than dictating the decision to them.

Finally, we as fathers must encourage, introduce, inform, and inspire a relationship between our sons and *the* Son, Jesus Christ. Whenever I drop nuggets of wisdom on my sons, I work to include insights about the affectionate love God has for each of us. I hope that I have inspired my children by letting them see me praying, reading, and teaching the word of God. I hope that I am demonstrating my zeal for a personal relationship with God.

After all, how can we know the rules of engagement if we won't read the rule book—that is, the Bible? There is nothing new under the sun, as articulated in this book, so it would befit us to take a peek to see what has been left for us here.

SEVEN NUGGETS OF EXPERIENTIAL SAGACITY

Life lessons meet
at the corner of
gratitude and
inner peace.

*You are set apart for good relational
health, good financial health,
and good personal health.*

You are special.

You were specifically and uniquely made, and there is no other person made exactly like you. When you become self-aware enough to know you are special, your flight path is different. You're flying at a higher altitude, with less disturbance than at ground level, less traffic than at ground level, and a much faster speed than at ground level. From there, you begin to see the world as it is.

Ray Dalio founded one of the largest hedge funds in the world and is reported to have a net worth of more than fourteen billion dollars. Bill Gates once said of Dalio, "He has provided me with invaluable guidance and insights." Both of these men are clearly set apart, with relationships in politics, economics, and technology. Could you imagine a plain ole transactional relationship feeling "invaluable" for these two titans of our era? I personally cannot. These two individuals recognize the value of collaborative relationships and the significant impact they make on our society.

People who are set apart understand the value of quality, healthy relationships. Regrettably, relationships are often seen as transactional. Meaning, there is always a deal to be made or some level of expectation to be met. It is an interaction with strings attached—the classic notion of, "I scratch your back, you scratch mine." There are conditions to the engagement. On the other hand, quality relationships are transformational, with both parties sharing respect for its value.

My relationship with my mother was truly set apart. Before her passing in 2020, we buzzed each other every morning at roughly 7 a.m., bantering comedically as we discussed the previous day's happenings. But more than that, whenever she or I faced challenges and issues in life, we leaned on each other as a sounding board to make more clear-eyed decisions. As she slowly and peacefully slipped away to eternity, I was right there by her side.

Some of my relationships date back many years, and the vast majority of my relationships are with folks that are more than ten to twenty years older than me. We still make time to meet face to face, sit and have a meal, and fellowship with one another. We'll check in on each other's family, talk through our respective business moves, and provide each other with feedback. These relationships are open and transparent. They embrace intellectualism for growth, inspiration, and motivation. They are encouraging yet honest with feedback. They are supporting, and they are challenging.

People who are set apart are solid stewards of their financial health. Your bank accounts and investments are a direct indicator of your financial wellness. Some simple principles of healthy financials: Number one, focus on your craft or skill in order to earn good money in your primary role as well as other sources of income. Second, save more than you spend. Buy more assets (things that appreciate in value) and hold fewer liabilities (things that depreciate in value). Unless you are truly skilled at playing the short-term investment game and have the time to follow the markets minute by minute and hour by hour, your best bet is to invest in financial instruments with long-term time horizons. Pursue slow and steady cumulative growth. Pay bills on time.

It is also important to maintain good credit, as this is how the American financial system functions. It is designed to weed out those who are not credit worthy from opportunities. In this way, being cash rich is not always enough. It takes cash, credit, and investments all working together. Likewise, maintain life insurance for the purpose of your offspring and loved ones who depend on you. Once your financial house is in order, give to such causes that you are passionate about and that are bigger than you.

Oftentimes, financial health requires a self-imposed aspect of delayed gratification. Enjoy some of your money, but not at the risk of becoming financially ill. This seems uncomplicated, but it is difficult to do. Being set apart means you handle and manage finances vastly differently from others. The model you set for others through your financial discipline is that of an unburdened life, not limited by debt or obligations to others. You become the lender and not the borrower.

People who are set apart understand that maintaining good personal health will cost you, in a good way. There is a cost to exercising on a regular basis. There is a cost to eating healthy. There is a cost to visiting a family doctor and a dentist on a regular basis. But the benefits cannot be overstated.

A few years ago, during my annual doctor's visit, when my primary care doctor ordered my labs as usual, I had a slightly elevated A1C for the first time ever. Also called a glycohemo-globin test or a hemoglobin A1C test, an A1C is a blood test that finds your average blood sugar level over the past two or three months. If you have diabetes, this test is done to see how well your diabetes has been managed recently, and the doctor uses this information to adjust treatment, if needed. If you don't, it is used to check for signs of prediabetes. Because diabetes has permeated my family's health history, I had a decision to make. Did I carry on with eating what I wanted to eat and drinking what I wanted to drink, or did I listen to my doctor's orders to curtail my consumption of sugary products?

The decision was easy for me, for two reasons. First, the thought of not being on this earth to walk, talk, and spend time with my children's children was simply not an option, at least as far as I have some level of control. Second, it would be imprudent for me to continue on as usual, without some level of discipline, and then to depend on others once the conse-quences of my own lack of discipline set in. The disciplined side of me won, and I immediately started to change my eat-ing habits.

Over time, through our own neglect or through genetics, our health can be compromised. If adverse health conditions are related to genetics, then it is best to see a doctor on a reg-ular basis to monitor and manage the issue. If the issues are within our control, we must adapt to prevent or reverse them. Far too often, I see and hear about men neglecting to go to the doctor for healthcare checkups. People who are set apart are doing preventative maintenance with annual check-ups, exer-cising, and eating healthy as much as possible.

Good health takes work, and you are set apart for both the work and the reward. For the quality of life you are set apart to have, taking good personal care of health is paramount. Health truly is wealth.

Happiness is overrated;
seek peace instead.

Happiness is a great feeling. I am happy when family is around. I am happy when I am watching sports in person or on television. I am happy when my favorite dish is being prepared, when I travel to different cities and different countries, when there is time to serenade myself with a good action movie. I am happy when I am fully healthy, and I am happy when I am earning lots of money. Unfortunately, there is a conclusion, a finality, a crescendo, to each of the aforementioned experiences. That means happiness is conditional. If I am not experiencing things like these, then my disposition or my mood is no longer happy. The euphoria of happiness lasts but for a moment of time.

By contrast, the gift of inner peace is linked to a spiritual state of being. My inner peace is not defined by the ebbs and flows of experiences and events around me. As mentioned earlier, my mother would say to me and others that I was the most unconcerned person she knew. I think my mother perhaps did not know how to articulate my behavior in this way, but as I contemplate my demeanor as a child, I believe I have always had some level of peace, no matter what was happening around me.

Peace is a goal well worth striving toward. What we focus on gives rise to peace or misery. In this regard, I try to mind my own business and stay out of others'. For those circumstances and situations I cannot control, I lead with prayer. When people and things disrupt that inner peace and disconnect that spiritual state of being, then we must evaluate whether there is a need to detach ourselves from these people and things. Going a step further, our mental health sometimes depends on this need to detach.

As it relates to *people* disrupting our peace: some losses are good losses. Toxicity emanates from certain individuals in our orbit—those who tend to upset or disrupt our inner peace. Naturally, it is difficult to handle when people we love or who we like walk away; however, I have learned that our identity is not tied to who walks away. The identity maker is the Lord God himself. The sun shines brighter when you know who you are and whose you are. When people walk away from you because of the unnerving degree of peace that emanates from you, let them walk. Some losses are good losses.

As it relates to *things* disrupting our peace: some losses are good losses. Let's take social media, for example. I will say at the outset that not all social media is bad. However, a good majority of it disrupts my inner peace. I am not one who needs a chunk of "likes" to validate my self-worth. I am not one who spends a lot of time scrolling through social media pages to see what people are doing, where people are going, and what people are wearing. I realized early that my mental health was too high a price to pay for little to no return. Therefore, outside of what is required for business, I have almost zero social media footprint. I have zero tolerance for it, choosing instead to limit my own exposure as I strive each day to reach that place of peace. Whether or not you are on social media, try to avoid giving disruptive, nonspiritual things more mental real estate than you can afford.

When a person reaches the pinnacle of inner peace, they can maintain a consistent state of gratefulness, thankfulness, and calm—regardless of the peaks and valleys, the ups and downs, the calamity of human-related storms. We only have so many days on this earth, we must use the time wisely. When things take too much valuable time and space, potentially disrupting your peace, some losses are good losses.

Earn the right to rest.

Over the years, my offspring often heard me repeating the words, "Business before pleasure." Not in the literal sense of business, but rather focusing on the completion of the task or activity at hand. You don't start and stop tasks or activities, and you certainly don't procrastinate.

Recently, I collaborated with a colleague to develop a strategy for the delivery of long-term services. The supplier was one of the most difficult counterparts to negotiate a multi-year deal with, but they had specific skill sets we needed to move our business along. When my colleague saw the difficulty ahead of us in getting a deal done, he backed out. I, on the other hand, saw the long-term benefits for the company, and I stayed with it. After more than eight months of negotiations, we landed on a long-term contract. This led to an unexpectedly significant financial reward, and with that, I could rest well, knowing that the company was in good contractual standing with the supplier for several years to come.

Seeing things through to completion goes back to being a person who stands by their word and rises to meet the moment by delivering on commitments and obligations. Work ethic is a state of mind. Take basketball great Kobe Bryant as an example. Within his sport of choice, Kobe Bryant did not have the greatest vertical (jumping) capability, he did not have the best dribbling skills, he was not the tallest, and he was not even the best basketball shooter. However, he loved competition at every level. And what he did have was the best work ethic among his peers and colleagues.

Kevin Garnett, an opponent and colleague of Kobe Bryant's, said the following of Kobe's work ethic:

"His relentless pursuit of excellence was inspiring to him and other players in the league."

"He never stopped striving for perfection and would push himself to the point of exhaustion, always looking for ways to get better."

"His approach to training and game preparation was second to none, and that he would always be well-prepared for every game."

"His unwavering dedication to his craft is what set him apart from other players and made him one of the greatest of all time."

You may not feel like completing a task or delivering on a commitment. Notwithstanding, people who have a good work ethic understand it's not about how you feel. It is about what must be done.

I admired my mother for her consistent ability to work extremely hard. I do not ever recall her complaining about having to work, either; she just did what she had to do. As I watched her example, she inspired me to do the same. Today, I am indeed no stranger to hard work. No matter what effort is involved, no matter how big or small, if I am engaged and committed to it, then I will get it done. All deference to my mother for teaching me the value of a good work ethic.

Finally, I should also note that resting on past accomplishments is undeniably a way to give less than your best, seeing no need for continuous improvement or growth. However, what I completed and accomplished yesterday was yesterday. Today is a new day, and I press on towards the mark of seeing new tasks, activities, and goals through to completion.

Along my journey, I have discovered a few things about expectations. One of which is that expectations can be a haven for disappointment and frustration. This is especially true when we have not properly communicated what we need, want, or desire from another person.

Communication is the centerpiece of expectations—it is unreasonable to expect anything without clear and proper communication. I cannot count how many times I have heard the following phrases, which is probably the same for many of you; "I expected her to do this..." "I expected him to do this..." "I expected him or her to complete this or that." But it is unreasonable to think that any human being can meet our expectations without us clearly communicating them first.

In the workplace, we set goals and performance metrics so that our expectations for the delivery of those goals and performance metrics can be met. It would be unreasonable to expect employees in the workplace to deliver on uncommunicated goals and performance metrics. The same tenet goes for a marriage; uncommunicated expectations are one of many sure-fire ways to catapult a marriage to unhealthy degrees. No matter how many years of marriage are at play, it is unreasonable to expect spouses to read minds.

Managing expectations carries a sense of reciprocity, where there should be a clear and realistic understanding of what is to be accomplished, achieved, and acceptable among all parties involved. Having had the great fortune to lead scores of people in corporate America really helped me grow in this area. I grew in the workspace and in my personal life. I learned that not everyone could or would handle matters as I would, so I had to communicate my expectations according to the capabilities of the person or people I was engaging.

Another thing I have discovered about expectations is that you cannot have expectations of others that you do not hold for yourself, period. I might push some buttons on this next set of examples, though they are only meant to highlight the point I am making. If a team has to work through the evening to meet a deadline set by leadership, how could the leader expect their team to deliver on that late evening if that leader leaves early to enjoy a nice meal and relax? How could a spouse expect a spouse to work themselves to death—figuratively, or sometimes not figuratively—whilst the other sits in the comfort of complacency? Having expectations of others and without having the same introspective expectations is outright inconsiderate and the height of hypocrisy.

To be clear, I am not saying that there has to be an externally equal level of contribution in any marriage or relationship; what I am saying is that there must be clear communication of what both parties want and need. What I have learned overall is I must clearly communicate what I need or what I want—within a reasonable portion of reality—so that I, personally, do not carry a constant spirit of frustration and disappointment.

When I was younger and participating in athletics, particularly basketball, I expected to be great. However, I did not put in the body of work to justify such expectations. As such, I was unable to blame someone else for my shortcomings in this area. When I did not get the athletic scholarship I had imagined receiving, I realized the lack of opportunities in this space rested with me. My own lack of commitment and lack of focus were to blame. By setting expectations for myself, there was clearly no one else to get frustrated or disappointed with. The buck stopped with me—and thus, my basketball career ended.

This reflective learning allowed me to provide the same insight to my children if they expected to be great at anything without putting in the required body of work. I often relayed to my children that I could cultivate the environment for them to be great in whatever they desired to do; however, I could not do the work for them. That part was their job.

I started journaling much too late in my view—not until my 40s, when so many people were coming to me for advice and insight on so many different topics. I started taking notes of my thoughts and insights, then turned those notes into inspirational quotes to send to my immediate family. Earlier in the book, I spoke about the significance of exposure for growth and development. Going a step further, journaling or taking copious notes of your memorable experiences, exposure, and unique thoughts throughout your personal life and career provides you with a look back on the evolution of your journey from boyhood to manhood.

Keeping a journal over the years has given me a window of opportunity to see who I am and what I value. Capturing my thoughts on paper also gave me the time to share, uplift, and encourage others. On some of my days in the valley, I even pulled on my previous writings to encourage myself.

I have become a voracious reader over the years, and I am truly inspired by authors who take the time to share their thoughts and ideas. It is a marvel to see the uniqueness and ingenious eloquence of the written word, knowing the effort that goes into that outcome. Robert Greene, author of *The 48 Laws of Power*, recently mentioned in an interview that it has taken him five years to finish his current book *The Law of the Sublime.*[17] The meticulous nature of writing is a gift that authors give to the world at large.

Take, for example, the Bible. The greatest collection of material ever written, dating back more than 2000 years—and without it, we would not understand what is on God's mind or His plan for humanity. These Biblical artifacts have shaped spiritual, intellectual, and moral frameworks for many centuries. Whilst I had never imagined writing a book at this level in my younger years, the copious notes that I had taken became instrumental for many of the concepts and thoughts that guided me through this writing. I believe my God-given gift, at least in part, is inspiring and motivating others toward growth and development. Whenever I am in the valley from my own personal challenges and circumstances, I try not to stay there too long, lest I become ineffective at this gift that I've been granted.

The journaled compilation of my unique thoughts, along with writing this book, helps cement my goal of leaving a legacy of written word for my children's children. Why is legacy so important to me? I have concluded with high hopes that it will help the generations that succeed me to extract at least a little of their history, the lineage of who they are.

Everyone has been given a natural endowment of their own thoughts and ideas. When the time is right for you to share those thoughts and ideas through various forms of communication, and especially through the written word, you just may inspire, enlighten, entertain, or bring others from the edge of despair.

Let me first start by naming what confidence is not. Confidence is not loud. It is not arrogant. It is not boastful. It is not prideful, dogmatic, hateful, or malicious. Merriam-Webster defines confidence this way:

a) *"a feeling or consciousness of one's powers and reliance on one's circumstance,"* b) *"faith or belief that one will act in a right, proper, or effective way."*

When certainty is combined with confidence, it yields a uniquely charismatic person.

What do I mean by certainty? You know who you are, whose you are, and what you value. When you know who you are, that sense of self will not allow for disrespect or belittling, either from your hand or at the hands of someone else. When you know whose you are, with a clear understanding that you are a child of the most high God—well, I can drop the mic right there. When you know what you value, when there are firm elements to life that you hold near and dear, there are unambiguous lines you will not cross. They become sacred attachments to your identity.

One of the reasons I enjoy sports is because of the level playing field it upholds. For me, it is more than just a pastime. It is a depiction of the level of work an athlete puts in, which builds that level of uncompromising confidence. The more hours the athlete commits to over and above the competition, the more confidence is reflected at game time. Unlike the workplace, academia, or politics, sports puts your commitment on display, in full transparency.

In the workplace, there is always the opportunity for nepotism; that is, the power and influence to favor family, friends, associates, and people who look just like you. In academia, there is the opportunity to admit students based solely on subjective criteria, not to mention the added advantages of legacy admission. On the political side, there is the opportunity for laws to favor one group of people versus another. In sports, it is only you versus your opponent or your team versus your opposing team. The confidence in skill, preparation, and studying will become evident on the field and on the court. No one can take away what you, yourself have put into your craft—not with bias, legacy, or gerrymandering.

Many people will try their best to define you when you do not fit their model of who you should be. Once, I was new to a project that had a mandate to deliver an enormous newly built gas-to-liquid plant. There were a few hundred staff supporting the effort, and my role was to develop the procurement strategy for the air-separation unit portion. It included working with other subject matter experts to develop the scope of work, establishing the pricing scheme, and engaging the supplier market, among other things. In order to understand the sheer magnitude of this role, you should know that the air-separation unit was expected to cost nearly a billion dollars. Yes, a billion dollars—and I had the responsibility to drive the procurement strategy that would get it built within the allotted schedule.

I first developed a rapport with critical staff such as the project manager, project services manager, safety manager, engineering managers, and legal team. Six months in, we were nearing the end of the year and the accompanying performance review time. As is normally the case, the supervisor would schedule your review, then you would meet to discuss what you did well, what you could do to improve, and what contributions you made that were outside of your role.

When it was time for my review, I walked into my supervisor's office with my pressed white shirt, tailored slacks, and a big wide smile as usual. I knew I was moving the strategy along well. The discussion started off really well, then slowly started to turn in a direction I had not prepared for. He said, "You are doing well, but there is one issue with you. You operate too much in the black and white—you need to learn to operate in the grey."

I was stunned.

He meant that if I needed to aggrandize things for the strategy to get approved in preparation for my competitive tender, I needed to be able to "operate in the grey" in order to proceed. Needless to say, I could not take this advice. I was and am certain of who I am and what I value; I could not allow a supervisor to define me. Notoriously being misunderstood throughout my nearly three decades in the energy business, there were more than a few instances wherein my reputation suffered when I refused to make decisions to fit a narrative other than who I was.

To be clear, a genuine critique of what I can do to improve is an invitation for my growth. But whenever feedback crosses the line of my value system, it is not for me. Further, the procurement strategy I had developed was approved without the need for me having to "operate in the grey," as it were.

As I have shared with many young men, including my two boys: keep your head held high, your shoulders back, and walk with intention. When one has continuously worked to consistently sharpen their craft and develop their certainty, they carry a natural hallmark of charisma. That type of charisma inspires, motivates, and elevates others. A charismatic person shifts the environment around them with their underlying tone of excellence and incessant improvement. When you are in a room—any room—own it. Be yourself. Be certain of who you are and whose you are. Your confidence is your choice.

Seek God's hand.

Seeking assistance is one of the most powerful demonstrations of humility. Asking for God's hand is much like asking for a neighbor's hand to lift a heavy object, asking for your partner's hand to open a jar, asking for a friend's hand to solve a complex math problem, or asking for a dad's hand to fix a bicycle. Although, God's hand carries much more power and authority. There is humility in each of these requests, as the individual must acknowledge that the task cannot be accomplished without assistance. It is also a way to showcase the support of the relationship in question. There is a better chance of getting that assistance when a relationship abounds.

As a parent, I could imagine my child coming to me for assistance with homework, to fix a bike, or any other request. Because my child recognizes me as having the capability to help solve the problem, my heart and my mind turn towards them to either grant the request or guide them to what is required. What more can we expect from God when we seek His hand to lift and cover our lives and provide assistance when we are incapable of solving our own problems? If my arrogance and pride get in the way of seeking God's hand, then I will be subject to an outcome that may or may not be favorable. I would much rather be in God's hand than my own at any and all stages of my life.

The artistry of seeking God's hand is not sophisticated. It is actually a rather simple process, simply to yield to that spirit of humility and petition God for His hand of guidance. Over the years that I have prayed, seeking God's hand on my life, there have been many tests, losses, and trials. From growing up in the rough-and-tumble public housing, to holding court using my fist for justice, pushing the edges, going through a divorce, and being on the receiving end of racial insensitivity, God's hand was ever-present through it all. Partly because I was active in seeking His hand, but more than that, because of who He is.

"Before a word is on my tongue, you, Lord, know it completely. You hem me in behind and before, and you lay your hand upon me." (Psalms 139: 4-5)

I hope the stories that I have shared in these pages demonstrate the truth that we all have the ability to weather the storms and struggles we face. I hope this book will become the kind of trusted resource that I could have used to draw strength from in those times when I could have used an extra boost of hope and insight.

My struggles, my challenges, and my trials may be different than yours. Even so, the reminder I want to leave for us all is that troubles don't last. The breakthrough starts when we are still long enough to listen for the answer to our petition, lean into our issues with confidence, and then become resilient enough to see it through to the other side.

Notes

1   Sanja Gupta, MD, *Keep Sharp* (Simon & Schuster, 2021), 46-47.

2   Dharius Daniels, *Rational Intelligence* (Zondervan: 2020), 102.

3   Mehdi Hassan, *Win Every Argument: The Art of Debating, Persuading, and Public Speaking* (Henry Holt and Company, 2023), 22.

4   Simon Sinek, "Trust versus Performance", YouTube, November 2020.

5   Wikipedia, "About Eleanor Roosevelt, October 1884–November 1962."

6   "Nelson Mandela: Beyond the Myth", Documentary, 2019

7   Mehdi Hassan, *Win Every Argument: The Art of Debating, Persuading, and Public Speaking* (Henry Holt and Company, 2023), 26.

8   Cal Newport, *Deep Work: Rules For Focused Success In a Distracted World* (Hachette Book Group, 2016), 17.

9   Sarah Payne, "The Economic Impact of Prison Labor for Incarcerated Individuals and Taxpayers," *The Princeton Legal Journal*.

10 Wikipedia, "John Cornelius Stennis, August 1901–April 1995".

11 Timothy Snyder, *On Tyranny: Twenty Lessons from the Twentieth Century* (Penguin Random House; 2017), 88.

12 Wikipedia, "September 11 Attacks, September 11, 2001."

13 Don Clifton, *Discover Your Clifton Strengths* (Gallup Press, Clifton Strengths version 2021).

14 John Bevere, *Good or God?: Why Good Without God Isn't Enough* (Palmer Lake Co: Messenger International Inc., 2015), 74.

15 David R. Hawkins, *Power vs. Force* (1st Hay House printing; 2013), 149.

16 Bruce Wilkinson with David Kopp, *The Prayer of Jabez* (Penguin Random House, 2000).

17 Codie Sanchez, "The Big Deal Podcast", YouTube, April 2025.

About the Author

Carnell Moses is a business leader and entrepreneur with three decades of experience in the energy industry, having negotiated multi-million-dollar deals all over the world as well as serving as CEO of an intermodal transportation company in the contiguous United States. Carnell earned an MBA from the University of St. Thomas in Houston, Texas and a bachelor's degree from Southern University and A&M College in Baton Rouge, Louisiana. He is a proud husband, father, and grandfather who actively serves his community, grateful for a lifetime of opportunities to mentor young men, practice servant leadership, and create employment for others.